Prai.. ...

The Promise of Soul Love

This deeply personal story of healing beyond the grave touches all our lives, whether we've experienced the dark waters of addiction or not. We're taken on a journey with many twists and turns, in search of love, self-worth and security. Ultimately, we're gifted by the words of wisdom from those in spirit who, having sought forgiveness, share the values of honesty, compassion and hope.

Christine Page, MD
Author of *The Heart of the Great Mother*

Pam Culley-McCullough has written a rich and evocative true story that captures all that is possible when we open ourselves to the enormity of spirit. With heartfelt candor, personal humility, and tender grace, *The Promise of Soul Love* takes the reader from a darkened world of alcoholic wounding, emotional pain and personal limitation to a transcendent capacity for hope, connection and universal light. These deeply moving pages abound with wisdom, clarity, and most importantly, heart-to-heart sharing. They invite the reader to expand our understanding of timeless relationships and to embrace the many ways that we can meet and heal the challenges of the human condition through the vehicle of love. A beautiful message for us all.

Jan Berlin, Ph.D.
Clinical Psychologist

Poignant, compelling, courageous, stunningly authentic and transparent in its touching into truth, *The Promise of Soul Love* reads like a memoir, but it is so much more – a beacon light of hope illuminating how to open up to life, Spirit, life after life, and eternal soul love, and in doing so heal yourself, your ancestors, and the world.

In telling her story and the story of her family, Pam Culley-McCullough describes a path of transformation that will break open your heart to see unlimited possibilities as you answer the call of your soul to heal even the deepest wounds in your life. She reassures us that with a willing heart, healing can always happen.

Lilia Shoshanna Rae
Author of *The Art of Listening to Angels*

Pam Culley-McCullough's book *The Promise of Soul Love* is an intimate story of a multi-generational family that struggled with alcoholism and the damage it causes. But it is also a love story, between Pam and her father and the gift of second chances at relationship, love and understanding. I felt like she was telling my story, and to know that I am not alone, and that others have triumphed over addiction, gives me hope and makes me happy. Pam writes clearly and brings everything to light. The beauty of the relationship with her father today shows me healing comes in many ways. I know you will love her book.

Susanne Romo, MBA
619-200-3594 Cell
CA P&C, LHD License #0720743
Sales Success Coach
Pipeline Insurance

What a joy it was to travel the twists and turns of the healing journey with Pam and Poppy as they discover together the experience of pure love that is possible for each of us no matter how challenging our family life is and was. I couldn't put it down! Pam so honestly shares her story and the lessons learned that it demonstrates to us that we too can heal any relationship even after our loved one passes. She assures us that communication with our loved ones doesn't end, it simply changes form. I feel inspired, as I'm sure you will be too, to find a clearer heart-to-heart Spirit-guided connection and exchange with loved ones who have passed. Ultimately, we discover the healing is for our true Self and the awakening of our soul's calling to love and be loved. Find encouragement and support as you read this beautiful work.

Rev. Cathy Silva
Relationship Transformation Author and Coach
Cathysilva.org

Whether your life has been surrounded by addiction, as was true in Pam's life, or whether you have experienced other difficult traumas, Pam's story encourages you to not lose hope, but instead see the higher calling in the challenge. It just may be calling you to embrace something that can lead to an extraordinary discovery.

Rev. Wendy Craig-Purcell
Founder and Spiritual Leader
The Unity Center in San Diego

Pam's unique voice gives the reader a glimpse into her relationship with her dad even though he has birthed into spirit. The love they share is a story of hope and courage that will touch your heart and soul.

This book is a groundbreaking book in many ways. Her connection to her dad and the world of spirit is inspiring. It creates a pathway so we too may know the power of love even after physical death. In many ways Pam's dad is doing what he had not done for his daughter while he was alive on earth. He is showing her unconditional love and in the end isn't that what most of us are searching for?

Katye Anna
Teacher Of Soul
www.katyeanna.com

Raw truth, Revelation and Redemption:
With awe-inspiring courage, Pam Culley-McCullough offers hope to those caught in the web of alcohol addiction, showing us how we can overcome negative effects of this disease and find deep healing beyond our physical world. The impact of *The Promise of Soul Love* is transformative, filled with unexpected outcomes, and is a must-read for anyone in a 12-Step program. Humanity needs this book now!

Linda Roebuck
Visionary Leader, Transformational Author
and Spiritual Mentor
Composer of *Circular Leadership, Together We Rise*
www.lindaroebuck.com

I consider *The Promise of Soul Love: Unexpected Gifts from Here and Beyond* far beyond a memoir!

Through her book, Dr. Pam Culley-McCullough takes us with her on a decades-long roller coaster ride with family and loved ones who struggled with alcoholism and betrayal. Powerful, thought-provoking and inspiring, her story provides hope for anyone who has been on a similar journey. I consider this a road map with insights and a guide in moving through to find that even in death, it's possible for healing and forgiveness to occur with passed loved ones!

Dr. Pam demonstrates that "Death won't part you. Your relationship will continue, just in a different form," as she moves into hope, healing, forgiveness, love and reconnection with departed family members. I highly recommend this book to anyone who has participated in or has a loved one in any of the 12 Step programs and I will be happily recommending and sharing her book with my clients and colleagues!

Rev. Gary Nobuo Niki
Shamanic Samurai Medicine Man,
Anger Management Facilitator &
Spiritual Counselor
Author of *d.i.y. zen* and *The Art of Gentle Emotional Transformation*

The Promise of Soul Love is an essential read! A story of recovery and supreme love. Pam Culley-McCullough opens up to us and illustrates the impossible is possible in forgiveness of the harshest blows in life. A traumatized child of an alcoholic father and a depressed mother, she heals and redeems her bond with them despite all odds. She returns to love with conventional community support, and much to her surprise, through a new and mysterious ability that radically changes her life: vivid communication with her father and others in spirit. A child of war, I also realized an ethereal gift to heal and to serve the world. I know the courage it takes, and I know the reward. This heartening book ignites hope. It reignited mine and brings me to more joy again.

Iva Nasr
Mentor, Speaker and Author of
From Guns to Roses—Memories and Miracles

There is nothing that stands in the way of Soul Love! Pam's memoir chronicles her father's and family's journey from abuse, alcoholism, and emotional pain to surrender and acceptance of something bigger than our human selves—an emergence into the spirit and the Soul where love is all there is. You will love the heartfelt story that unravels the secrets her family kept during periods of great strife during the Great Depression and into modern day America, including Pam's own discoveries and secrets about her mediumship abilities to receive messages from loved ones in the spirit world. This beautiful memoir shows us that love transcends all, even death, as Pam tells this magnificent story with the help of those passed on into the spirit world, including her father, mother, and other loved ones of the Culley family. It takes courage to speak your truth, but in doing so, as Pam writes in her memoir, you liberate your Soul, allowing love to heal all wounds. I hope you take the journey with Pam in a story that will warm your heart and open you to what Pam's father, Cliff, calls 'your Highest Power.' Reading this book will bring you *The Promise of Soul Love*, exactly as written in the book title.

Anumani Santos
Modern Day Shaman
Award-winning author, artists, channel,
Speaker and spiritual mentor

The Promise of Soul Love, Unexpected Gifts from Here and Beyond is a page-turner, offering wisdom and love throughout. It is a guide to exploring the possibilities of connection for healing through Spirit, even after death. It offers hope for those who are grieving their deepest losses. Pam's words offer comfort and support throughout, promising us that we can continue deepening our soul love connections with those here and in spirit. Don't miss out on the opportunity to invite this in. Pam's words show you the way.

Helen M. Sherry, Ph.D.
Spiritual Intuitive and Transformational Guide
www.LiveandGrow.com

The Promise of Soul Love

A Memoir

UNEXPECTED GIFTS FROM HERE AND BEYOND

PAM CULLEY-MCCULLOUGH

THE PROMISE OF SOUL LOVE
Unexpected Gifts from Here and Beyond

PUBLISHING

Published by:
Capucia, LLC
211 Pauline Drive #513
York, PA 17402
www.capuciapublishing.com

Paperback ISBN: 978-1-945252-90-7
eBook ISBN: 978-1-945252-91-4
Library of Congress Control Number: 2020917710

Cover Design: Ranilo Cabo
Layout: Ranilo Cabo
Editor and Proofreader: Corinne Dixon
Book Midwife: Carrie Jareed

Printed in the United States of America

The Promise of Soul Love

A Memoir

UNEXPECTED GIFTS FROM HERE AND BEYOND

To Source and Soul for its loving insistence
that I follow this path.

Contents

Introduction

For the past twelve years, my dad, Poppy, and I have been creating what you are about to read, with me here and him in spirit. What you will experience is a collaboration of our efforts to highlight the importance of healing from what we could while still together in the physical, while allowing the process (gnarly, at times) to take us closer to the true meaning of love and forgiveness.

The original idea to write a book together came solely from him. It was easy for him to imagine our collaboration. I, on the other hand, had mountains to climb. I was utterly intimidated by the notion. First, I lacked knowledge and experience as a memoir writer. As a psychologist, I had written many academic papers, but never a memoir. I soon learned the two required quite different skill sets. Once acknowledged, I realized I would become a student once again. Yet, by far the bigger obstacle was accepting the fact that I would share the very nature of our current relationship with a broader audience. For many years I had enjoyed a high level of comfort talking about my family's dance with addiction. I often shared this (when appropriate) with individual clients or in designated support groups for adult children from alcoholic families (ACA/ACOA). It was a force that had shaped my life like no other. Sharing how it challenged me, and how I healed along the way, helped facilitate clients' growth and, in turn, supported them in their own healing. But revealing the afterlife conversations that took place between my father and I was altogether different. I would need to publicly admit I could see and hear him even though he was no longer in physical form. I fretted over what my family, friends and colleagues might think of my sanity!

As you read, you will see my many moments of being overcome by fear followed by my ambivalence to come out of the "spiritual closet," as I saw it. However, these challenges would become part of my journey towards learning to trust this call, in addition to allowing myself to be supported by otherworldly energies, one of which was Poppy.

Our story took shape as we both offered ideas to one another. The process was easy. I wanted to know more about his early childhood beginnings, a topic he had kept secret throughout my childhood and early adult years. Seeking truth, I yearned for a more cohesive understanding of who he was. I had always viewed relationships through a psychological prism. Knowing all I could know about my dad's life was no exception. I wanted transparency. By doing so, I knew it would add to my understanding of my family; moreover, it would lend insight to some of the emotional legacies I had inherited. Poppy wanted to underscore the importance of not becoming a victim to adversity. He also wanted his recovery story to be central for readers to see. We both agreed to share about the mercurial nature of addiction in addition to recovery as it played out in our relationship. I wanted to highlight the struggles coupled with the patterns inherent for a child who lives alongside a parent's addiction — the evolution of codependency, loneliness, anxiety, depression, and over-functioning (or for some, under-functioning), not to mention the constant undercurrent of powerlessness that infiltrates one's self-worth. Lastly, Poppy wanted me to share his experiences just before and after his transition to spirit. He wanted others to see our willingness to be open to anything that would foster deeper healing for us both even though it was messy at times.

As I said earlier, Poppy had no qualms about openly sharing our afterlife conversations. He was deeply invested in others, knowing that love and healing have no boundaries, not even the death of the physical body; it is simply a transition from one dimension to another. He taught me that many souls in spirit want to help those of us still here (even if they had not been so helpful while alive); they long for ongoing healing for their loved ones as well as for their own evolution while in spirit. I have since learned from him that we choose our kinship families, along with the many challenges we may face together, as a result. He supported what I learned from ancient Native American teachings, saying every time we heal something within ourselves, we heal our families seven generations back and seven generations forward (perhaps even further). We both firmly believe that no matter what has challenged you, whether you know it or not, you have the power to heal and transcend it.

A surprising experience began to unfold as a result of my ongoing relationship to Poppy: my heart began to open to a more expanded awareness to receiving messages not just from him, but from others in spirit. The more I wrote parts of this story, the more I received messages from my relatives featured in the early chapters. They were so happy when I chose to share their voices from spirit to bring you closer to understanding their account of their own lives at the time. It was also very illuminating to me.

Once comfortable opening to my kinship family in spirit, I began to receive even more messages, this time from others beyond my own extended family (some known and some not known to me) who wanted me to communicate to their loved ones still here. Surprised at first, I slowly realized this path was showing me the way to my next calling...becoming a translator for those in spirit wishing to connect to their loved ones still here, along with loved ones here wanting further connection to family and friends who have transitioned to spirit.

I am amazed at how things unfolded to bring me to where I am. Never in a million years did I ever expect this particular path to emerge, calling me to stand firmly on it. Such a gift and such a blessing to be chosen to be a medium between this realm and the next to help facilitate healing between loved ones whenever needed.

When a condensed version of this story, entitled "The Gold in the Darkness," was published in 2015 in the anthology, *Pebbles in the Pond, Wave Four,* compiled by Christine Kloser, I created a website (pamculley-mccullough.com) and a blog (www.conversationswithpoppy.com) as a way to share some of Poppy's powerful teachings. His insights offer many an alternative view of what can happen once someone dies. I also created a private group on Facebook called "Afterlife Journeys" where I share some of the afterlife experiences I have with my mom (and others) who have helped me weather the numerous trials we all encounter being in human form. You may be interested in joining my community at some point. If so, I would love to hear from you. On my website I offer a free guided meditation called "Finding Peace Within," which you can easily download and enjoy. Feel free to access my website or contact me directly at pam@pamcmc.com.

Throughout the story I use the term Spirit to refer to a dimension or realm as well as an otherworldly energy. You may prefer to think of this energy as God, Mother/Father God, Divine Spirit, Great Spirit, Higher Power or Source, to name a few. Also, you may prefer to think of the spiritual realm as Heaven. Feel free to substitute whichever terms resonate for you, especially if my terminology does not feel comfortable.

Even though I called my dad Poppy for many of my adult years, I chose not to use his nickname in our story until our afterlife relationship began. It is simply a way to keep the nature of our relationship clear to you, the reader.

Now, it is time to bring forth the promise Spirit made to us just weeks before my dad made his transition to where it took us, how we learned about soul love's promise to transform the pain of the past in order to usher in a deep and abiding peace in the present.

Spirit's Promise

My dad slept quietly in the hospital bed in his living room as the sun set late one April afternoon. He did not have long to live. The hospice caregivers were gone for the day as I settled into my caregiver role for the evening. Cancer had had its way with his body even though he had followed the advice of oncologists for four years, never deviating from their trusted recommendations. It had given us time to make every minute count. Yet death was imminent. It signified our final goodbye. To keep that harsh reality at bay for just a moment longer, I started reading a meditation to myself about letting go from Stephen Levine's book, *Healing into Life and Death*, a constant companion at the time.

Once I finished and reflected on the passage, my dad woke. Despite his constant supply of morphine, he said in a very lucid tone, "Honey, I like that passage, too—the one about letting go."

Yes, I was reading about letting go. However, how had he known? Perplexed, I went over to his bedside to re-read the passage he said he liked as a way to double-check. "Yes," he said, "that's the one."

Realistically, we both knew this connection could not be happening, except it was. As shock and surprise reflected in our eyes, we suddenly felt an otherworldly energy surround us, telling us that indeed we were communicating, now telepathically, and we would continue to communicate in this way even after his death.

This story could begin with what appears to be the tragedy of Dad's pending death, or about the promise that Spirit brought us that evening. The fact is the story begins much earlier. Even though those early years had the makings of a tragedy, it is not a tragedy at all. Instead it is a story of love and redemption.

I was his daughter for 47 years, along with being his caregiver at the end of his life. Now I am his translator as he shares life as he knows it from another dimension.

Yet, how we got here is a contrasting story, neither a natural nor easy progression for us. Our early strong bond of love as father and daughter sat amidst the thorns of struggle. My longing for our hearts to be open to love, joy and laughter was met by the sting of those thorns; yet they became our teachers, forcing us to open to learning about the true meaning of love. Did we know this at the time? Not at all. Wounds from my dad's childhood as well as mine prevented much insight. Yet our souls quietly guided us, giving us the experiences we needed to accept Spirit's promise of an ongoing connection after death.

What were those wounds—those challenges we inherited and faced? Knowing this is central to understanding how very unlikely it would be for my dad and me to share what we have today. But it also shows how love can lead the way to experience what is most extraordinary...its healing power, whether in this life as we know it, or in the afterlife.

The story begins when the seeds of struggle were first planted in the soil of Dad's childhood, how they took root, eventually shaping many of the joys and challenges I would have as his daughter.

Family Members

Rebecca   Dad's paternal grandmother; my Culley great-grandmother

Charlie   Dad's father; my Culley grandfather

Alta   Dad's mother; my Culley grandmother

Sim   Charlie's brother; Dad's uncle

Muriel   Dad's older sister; my aunt

Herb   Dad's older brother; my uncle

Lila   Dad's youngest sister; my aunt

Maureen   A Culley cousin; one of Herb's children

Kathleen   A Culley cousin; one of Herb's children

Penny   A McCullough cousin; Mom's older sister's child

Michael   A McCullough cousin; Mom's younger sister's child

Dottie   My godmother

Wickie   My godfather

Edith   Mom's mother; my McCullough grandmother

The

Seeds of a

Legacy

Chapter 1

Prairie Beginnings

I am breathless as I run into the house after playing with Bruce and Barbara, the kids living next door. Bike-riding is one of our favorite activities. Today, it has happily filled my afternoon. I find my dad sitting in the living room reading, something he loves to do in his free time. My six-year-old self bounds over to him and plops down to sit next to him in his favorite chair. He always makes room for me. I love that about him. The large rounded padded arms of the chair give me extra room to lean on. I find myself fingering the chair's nubby texture, following the occasional gold thread woven into its tan fabric as I settle in. Glancing at what he is reading, I notice its tiny print and the absence of pictures. How can anyone like a book without pictures, I wonder? The "Dick and Jane" series of books I get to read in my first-grade class are always full of them.

My thoughts are interrupted when my dad puts his book aside, saying in his usual upbeat and friendly manner, "Hi Pammy-girl" (one of the many nicknames he has for me), what have you been up to?" With my excitement overflowing, the words spill out of my mouth, as I fill him in about my latest bike-riding stunts.

Then, unable to keep silent about what is really on my mind, I blurt out, "Bruce said his grandma and grandpa are coming for a visit in a few days." I pause for a moment, then ask, "Do I have a grandma and grandpa?" Dad hesitates, cautiously answering, "Yes.... you do." I notice his hesitation. Unsure what to do, I ignore it. Instead, I press on, asking, "When will they come to visit us?" It is his long pause that puts me on edge. He sits up in our shared chair, leaning forward, making it difficult for us both to remain snuggled together. Being small, I quickly move to perch myself on the arm of the chair. But gone is our usual easy-going mood. I notice the corners of his mouth subtly twitching, as he looks down at the patterned area rug under his feet. In a measured tone I notice his careful choice of words and answers, "It's unlikely. They all live far away." In short order, I realize there is something about *this question* that is definitely *not* OK to pursue.

Why, I wonder? What is it about this question that changes our openness? Feeling like I have done something terribly wrong, I go silent.

Still with nagging curiosity though, I go looking for answers from Mom. I find her in the kitchen making dinner. She stands over the white porcelain sink peeling vegetables, occasionally wiping her hands on her apron. Hesitating at the doorway, I look down at the flecks of color in the linoleum floor, deciding whether or not to interrupt her. My curiosity wins out.

"Hey, Mom, do I have a grandma and grandpa?" After giving me a fleeting glance, she returns to slicing the newly-peeled vegetables.

My sense that she does not want to be bothered grows when the lid of a pan she reaches for slides off, making a racket. She is definitely not happy now. She recovers, pretending otherwise. Even so, her voice gives away her irritation as she pointedly says, "You have a grandmother living in Illinois." Her emphatic tone tells me this needs to be the end of my questions. But I do not heed her warning. I want to know more. Bruce had said they have cousins visit when their grandparents come. I wondered if I also had cousins. I ask, feeling a knot slowly forming in my stomach. Briefly looking at me, she says bluntly, "Yes, of course you do! You have your cousins Penny and Michael." I remember Penny and Michael, although I had not realized they were considered cousins. I am not even sure what a cousin is, anyway. I just know I do not remember seeing them very often. Just as I consider asking Mom why, she interrupts my thoughts, saying in a clipped tone, "Tell your father it is time for dinner." I'm stunned. There is not anything my six-year-old self can think to say. My stomach tightens once again from the escalating tension. I know something is not right here; I am just not sure what it is. As we sit at the table eating dinner, I am immersed in my thoughts while my parents engage in their usual conversation about their friends and my dad's work. Remaining quiet in my own thoughts, one thing becomes clear: when I ask about family my parents' irritated reaction is soon followed by a wall of silence.

This episode, and others I experienced throughout my early years, made it clear that family history was to remain in the past, never to be discussed. When challenged, my parents would avoid looking at me, while trying to cover up their instant discomfort. Any words said were often vague, spoken in an off-handed way, as though my question was not the least bit important. Like many children, I picked up on their distress, over time allowing the very familiar knot that formed in my stomach to become my silencer.

Even though I longed to know who my relatives were, where my parents grew up, and what their families were like, the experience always taught me that my curiosity got me into a bind. Feeling like I was in trouble meant I was at fault. The belief I might be the cause of their painful silence was worse than the queasy feeling in my stomach. Helpless, I shut down, adopting their firmly-established code of silence well into adulthood.

Many years have passed since being silenced about my family's history. My dad and I have now committed to writing our story together. Contemplation has brought the realization that it is time to take a step back and begin to unlock some of the keys from Dad's past. I feel ready to discover more about his early years. I am determined to bring light to what was kept in the dark all these years. Basically, one simple wish fuels my desire: I want to know the truth. Sitting at my desk, I light a candle, opening to Poppy in spirit. Immediately, I feel his presence. "Poppy, there is so little I know about your early years. How do I begin to learn more?" Rather than hearing any words or having a dialogue, I feel his energy direct my attention to a box of old family photos, long-forgotten in the far corner of the room. I see the large tattered brown and beige shoe box, its original contents a new pair of hiking boots he likely purchased at one time (according to the sticker still attached). This box contains a lifetime of my dad's memories, still quite unknown to me.

I open the box, spreading the pictures out to view. Immediately, I am drawn to one in particular. It looks to be a picture of an old weather-worn homestead cabin. I have seen this picture before, although I cannot remember where. There is nothing written on the back to indicate how it fits into Dad's history. Poppy whispers, urging me to find the book about our ancestry completed by my cousin Kathleen just before his passing. I locate my copy, opening it to see this very picture, followed by the caption: "Post card to Miss Ruby Prest, Indian Valley, Idaho from your Loving Friend, Alta Culley." I read further as Alta (Dad's mother) writes to her friend Ruby from her first home in Sublette, Idaho ..."On the left-hand side is the kitchen and the other end the front room. Our bedrooms are upstairs. The white in front is snow and in the distance is sagebrush." At the bottom of the picture, Kathleen had added: "Dr. came from Burley, ID to this house (43 miles away) to help birth the children. Cliff (my dad), Herb and Muriel (his older siblings) were born here."

Dad's birthplace, homestead cabin in Sublette, ID.

I am stunned. No wonder Dad kept this picture. This was his birthplace in late August of 1918. If Kathleen had not identified this as my father's first home I would have guessed from the vintage of the photo, alongside the condition of the cabin, that it was instead the childhood home of one of my grandparents or even great-grandparents.

Shocked by Alta's description of the cabin, I cannot imagine a kitchen and a front room existing together in what looks to be a dwelling no larger than 10'x10'. Somehow it held a family of five. She must have been referring to a possible loft upstairs as the "bedroom." I wonder if they even had indoor plumbing or electricity. I see the lace curtains hanging in the two front windows, adding a contrasting touch of softness to the harshness of the surrounding prairie. Maybe it had been Alta's way of making this cabin a home.

I want to know more. I consult my cousin Kathleen while also conducting a Google search to get a feeling for this area. The town of Sublette is located in a rural area of southern Idaho, surrounded by sagebrush with the rolling hills of the Sublette Mountain range in the distance. Originally dominated by the lucrative fur trade of the 1800s, it had since become farm country. In the ten years prior to 1920, the population of Sublette had doubled to 15,000, making it desirable for families who wanted fertile land to farm as well as a place to raise their children.

What had brought Dad's parents to Sublette, I wonder? Census records show that Alta and Charlie were married for four years by the time Dad was born. Having three children in that span of time surely made steady employment crucial. When it came to earning a living, sadly, my cousin Kathleen along with her sister Maureen verify one of the few things I remember Dad telling me about Charlie when I was much older: he preferred reading a good book to earning a steady living.

Dad's mother, Alta, around 1914-1915. Age 16-17.

I feel Poppy's presence around me as I process his dad's aversion to work. His energy is unsettled and stormy. Using dark, swirling colors to illustrate this mood, he tells me there is more I need to investigate. Through continued research, I learn that Charlie had a past before he married Alta. This had not been his first marriage. He had married before in eastern Oregon, having two children (being raised by their mother) who were adolescents by the time he remarried (this time in Idaho) at the age of 36. Alta's marriage to Charlie made her a stepmother at the young age of 16.

Dad's father, Charlie, around 1925-1930. Age 48-53.

Already I feel a foreboding as the story slowly unfolds. Poppy shakes his head, showing me an image of his heavy heart, as I discover more of what begins to complicate his family history. Charlie is old enough to be Alta's father. I now ask Alta if she wants to share more of her story with me from spirit. She eagerly appreciates the opportunity. "*I was desperate to leave my troubled life behind and marry Charlie. I was terribly mistreated as a child. I rarely felt cared about or valued. I wanted nothing more than to leave as soon as I could. Charlie was dashing. He offered excitement along with marriage and a way out. I had high hopes."* My heart sinks as I sense her innocence coupled with her child-like desire to be rescued. I know this will likely not end well.

Despite Charlie's aversion to work, I learn he got interim employment as a farm manager. It is easy for me to imagine life with the increasing needs of this growing family, especially when my dad said he developed an allergy to cow's milk, making frequent trips to town essential for Charlie, to purchase enough goat's milk to soothe Dad's condition. This added expense came on top of the family's mounting needs. Compounding this was the fact that travel was not easy (still by horse and wagon for many) with the nearest towns spaced miles apart.

I learn Dad's family left Idaho within two years, possibly due to the situation in Idaho being inadequate to meet the growing family's needs. Yet it is more likely the move was prompted by the possibility of support available from extended family in the chosen destination: eastern Oregon, where Charlie spent had most of his childhood and early adult years. After having travelled more than 400 miles over part of what is now the well-established Oregon Trail Highway, this family of five arrived in the small town of Weston.

Weston and Umatilla County are home to many of my paternal ancestors. Early arrivals heeded the call of adventure beside their desire for a better life. They traveled by wagon train to what was then called "Oregon Country." By the mid-1880s, as Oregon became a newly-formed state, more of my family members came. This later migration included Charlie, his younger brothers, his parents and his maternal grandmother, all arriving from Missouri by overland train.

Weston is a community I came to know as a teenager. It is nestled at the foothills of the Blue Mountains, sitting on the banks of the winding Pine Creek. Maybe Dad's parents thought this was a better choice for their young family. I found provocative ads placed by the local Chamber of Commerce and the County Farm Bureau at the time, describing the area as: "surrounded by rich farming country offering thousands of acres of fertile land awaiting the coming home-seeker; an ideal climate wherein crops never fail; a sustainable dependable town whose people are friendly, thrifty, with business houses that are well-established and reliable." At the time, the town of 594 people boasted of excellent grade schools, a high school, paved streets, concrete sidewalks, and electric lights along with an ample supply of clean fresh mountain water. No sooner had I written this description when Poppy tells me how much he loved this area and the town of Weston. Brilliant pink color swirls around his heart as he says, *"Few people were strangers; it was home. I always felt I belonged there."* Even within these brief statements, I easily feel his deep love for this community.

Many of Charlie's relatives remained in Weston during the years Charlie lived in Idaho: his parents, brothers and a late-in-life sister. Alongside an extended family living in the surrounding area, a home-town atmosphere, I am hopeful I will discover that Weston holds promise for the family.

Family stories, however, point out the key to any measure of stability and success for Charlie comes from Uncle Sim, his capable business-smart brother. Always resourceful, Sim saw that Charlie had what was needed. He made sure the family had a place to live on the ranch he and his wife had inherited from her deceased parents (a place affectionately referred to over the years as the "Ranch House"). For the time being, Sim secured work for Charlie, once again as a farm manager.

Grandmother Rebecca (Charlie's widowed mother) became a steady force early on. Family stories said she helped Alta learn how to take care of her home, managing what few resources they had. Grandmother Rebecca was practical, sturdy and steady (values my dad greatly admired). She was someone Alta could count on. From spirit, Alta verifies this, adding: *"I felt loved by Grandmother Rebecca; she was the mother I never had. She cared about me in such a special way."* Grandmother Rebecca offers her thoughts, too: *"I loved Alta. She was full of life, but so poorly equipped to manage all it took to survive. She wanted more out of life, but little was in place to offer that."*

Now just 20, Alta was the mother of three children all under the age of five. From many accounts, she was described as a fun-loving young woman. Where was the fun in her life as her children's needs increased, I wondered? Charlie's disdain for work threatened financial jeopardy at every turn. Even more worrisome, and like his father before him, I learn Charlie has a propensity toward alcohol abuse.

"This is where the legacy begins, where alcoholism takes root in your family, right?" I say to Poppy in spirit. He confirms this truth, showing himself and his siblings surrounded by a whirlwind of chaotic energy. The image speaks volumes. He not only had a grandfather whose life was focused around alcohol, but a father, as well.

Family members tell me alcohol became the main way Charlie, and eventually Alta, managed their mounting frustrations. I hold both of them in my mind's eye, trying to imagine that time in their lives. Charlie's energy comes forward. He shows me a strong burst of steam spewing from the top of his head. I interpret this to mean drinking began as a way to blow off steam, which he verifies. The steam, however, turned into fury, eventually escalating into fights with Alta, he admits. He says the deep disappointment his father had in him now becomes what he believes as well. Alta soon joins in to share about her dashed dreams for a better life. She wanted to be loved, although part of her felt deeply unlovable, she reveals, admitting that drinking had provided an easy escape. *"I fought with Charlie to provoke him. I flirted with other men to show him how deeply disappointed I was in my marriage. It was all I knew to do."*

Tears well up in my eyes as I say to Poppy: "I'm so saddened by the effect drinking had on your early life. You witnessed your parents' frequent arguments along with the chaos it brought. I now understand why you kept silent over the years. As a child and young adult, I always felt an undercurrent of your unspoken anger and resentment. It would seep out sometimes, attaching itself to a seemingly benign situation. You would erupt over something small. Despite the craziness, did you ever feel loved or cared for by your parents?" As dark swirling colors circle his heart he says, *"I felt love, but it was fleeting. Early on, we knew we had to look out for ourselves. We frequently did what we could to get out of harm's way."*

In that moment, it all became clear. I fully comprehended how festering emotional pain coupled with the beginning of alcohol abuse in his parents' lives created my dad's early family trauma, for him and his siblings from an early age. My heart was heavy, feeling his pent-up anger on top of the deep sadness he seemed to carry for many years. I had tuned in to these feelings growing up, never knowing their source. Now, it began to make sense. Yet, as I persisted, linking his past to the present next to the man I had known as my dad, I was acutely aware this was just the tip of the iceberg. It was not surprising to learn more challenges would soon follow.

Chapter 2

Seeds of Struggle

"**P**oppy, here is a picture of you alongside your older brother and sister; you look to be about four years old. Who is the child sitting in the little chair in front of you with his feet barely touching the ground?" *"That's my uncle!"*

I vaguely remembered hearing from several Culley cousins that Dad had a younger uncle. Here was the proof. I investigate further by talking with Kathleen. The two-year-old little boy belongs to Alta's *parents*. He is their late-in-life child. They now have moved to the area from Idaho.

I wonder what this development suggests for Alta. She might have been happy to distance herself from her family at one time, but how would it have been to now have her parents closer along with a brother 23 years younger than she ... and younger than her *own children?* Alta gives me her perspective: *"I didn't think of anything beyond what was on the surface. My new brother kept me distracted from what was missing in my own life. I wanted to avoid anything messy even though I played a hand in it.*"

Various family commentaries from my cousins indicate troubles kept nagging Dad's parents. Competing needs along with their 20-year age difference seemed to have been central to the festering frustrations, compounded by their ongoing meager resources. Obviously, this had not been solid ground from which to build a stable and harmonious family environment.

Critical to the context of farm life is that it is all about being practical. Having a good work ethic ensured success, as did being resourceful. Everyone had to learn to make the most of what they had, no matter how meager. Winters in eastern Oregon were (and still are) relentlessly cold. A well-managed, productive farm ensured survival during the long winter months. If that were lacking, the reality was chillingly harsh.

Despite this grim picture, Dad's youngest sister, Lila, was born. Six years younger, she came into a family whose financial and emotional resources were stretched desperately thin. Poppy weighs in, saying, *"She was so vulnerable. While we were in school we couldn't keep our eye out for her. I hoped she was OK, but I always worried."*

*Dad (around age 10) seated next to his older sister Muriel with his brother
Herb, standing, and sister Lila.*

One of the things that had helped sustain the family, however, was their love of music and dancing. Alta was social and fun-loving. Charlie, although a bit more introverted, always liked a party. Some of my Culley ancestors were known to be good musicians, playing the fiddle, the piano, and singing. They performed at local square dances, often playing songs popular at the time like "Turkey in the Straw." Both of Dad's parents tell me from spirit they were in their element while singing, dancing and socializing, enjoying the release it brought them from their troubles. Nevertheless, alcohol, too, provided release, as they show me a scene played out in my mind's eye where they are both very drunk while in the throes of a full-fledged fight in the late hours of the evening. It brings chills to my body. Prohibition was in place at this time, although Oregon, especially eastern Oregon, rarely experienced it. The area became known as a bootlegger's paradise. It did not hurt that Charlie's parents managed the local hotel and bar in town at the time, likely ensuring a steady supply of alcohol for everyone. It was not surprising to see how Charlie and Alta's excessive drinking turned to addiction, just like it had for Charlie's father. For years, Charlie's father had been known as a "problem drinker" (code for alcoholic) and the issue had been considered a contributing factor to his premature death at age 50.

Remembering what Dad had painstakingly told me about the early recollections of his parents' fighting, it was easy to see how drinking turned Charlie and Alta into people who could barely function. The more they drank, the more they fought. The more fights they had, the more blows their fragile marriage sustained. Due to mounting disappointments and unmet needs, family stories indicated they both sought refuge in relationships outside of their marriage.

A defining moment (told to me by my cousin Maureen) came when Dad's brother Herb, about 12 at the time, came home from school one day, only to find his mother in bed with another man. As shocked and devastated as he was, he probably knew on some level where this would lead…it was not any place good.

This surely was a critical turning point in the marriage. There was no looking the other way, no pretending. There was no turning back. This was betrayal in its purest form. Emotions escalated once Charlie found out. In the heat of the moment, while Charlie and Alta unleashed their pent-up fury at each other, as Maureen tells it, Alta impulsively tugged at her wedding ring, forced it off of her finger, hurling it across the room in a rage. Her actions spoke volumes. She was tired of being mistreated by Charlie. She was tired of dashed hopes. She was simply overwhelmed by disappointments. She was done.

After 13 years of marriage, it was over. Alta left Charlie, moving to a neighboring state, and taking Dad's two sisters. She could not have known the unfortunate timing, since the most severe long-lasting economic depression this country had ever seen had just begun. It was 1929. Known as the "Great Depression," it brought most people, communities, and states to their knees. Few people had work. The bread lines were long. Day-to-day survival was the bottom line for most families. Having an eighth-grade education, this became her reality as Alta found the only work she could as a waitress. As I reflect on this situation my heart feels the effect of this new level of devastation to the family. All that remains is a gut-wrenching sense of despair.

My dad and his brother Herb remained living at the Ranch House with Charlie in Weston. As divorce loomed and their sisters and mother now 100 miles away, from spirit Poppy characterizes it as a dark time. He had wondered if he would ever see his sisters again, or even his mother. *"The whole town knew what happened. Everywhere we went we knew others knew about our parents' misguided, crazy behavior."* I mention the stigma often assigned to being a child of divorced parents at the time. *"Yes. We all felt it. What could we do about it?" I learned to keep my eyes forward, never to look back. That way I didn't have to feel the humiliation. I saw early on how my parents were deeply flawed."*

Sadly, Alta's mother suddenly found herself in similar circumstances to her daughter. Her husband of 30-plus years (Alta's father) left her for a younger woman with young children. He relocated with her, leaving Alta's mother to raise their youngest child, now nine, with little support. Strange as it was, mother and daughter found themselves in the same boat, both raising children alone. I could not help but wonder if the hardship would ever end for them or the family members involved. Slowly dawning on me was the fact that they were relatives, *my relatives*. People, who until now, had been strangers to me.

By now, the seeds of struggle had left Dad's family deeply splintered. For many years, the break-up of his family remained an unspeakable tragedy to him. Only during the last few years of his life did he speak of his fragmented family. He finally found a way to speak about his grave concern for his sisters' well-being, six-year old Lila in particular, and his worry that they, too, might be forced to marry early as their mother had done. Already so vulnerable, they might end up on the same path, one that he fretted would also include the destructive force of alcohol. His words at the time struck me deeply: "Alcohol… nothing good has ever come of it." In these times of sharing, I witnessed how exposure to his parents' volatility reinforced his tendency (as my dad) to speak in a deliberately measured tone, void of overt emotion. Poppy verifies this now from spirit. *"Removing emotion from my thoughts always helped me remain level-headed. I had no idea how much emotion I buried until I became sober. Even then, I couldn't heal the deeply buried pain until I made my transition to spirit."*

Any child would be upended by these tragic circumstances leaving them deeply vulnerable, and Dad had not been the exception.

However, true to his nature, he did not dwell on it. Out of this unwanted shameful situation came his determination to take charge of what he could. He would not be victimized by his past. He was a focused pragmatist.

Never having faced this experience, I had asked Dad in his later years how he found the strength to move forward. In his usual analytical fashion, he had simply commented, "I focused my attention where it counted most: school and sports. School was my refuge where I knew I could excel."

Weston's schoolhouse was a small, two-story brick building housing no more than 50 students. The Weston population was hovering around 600 people at the time, making it easy for my dad as well as Herb to know most of their classmates and families. What a godsend! Being in such close proximity, families began to provide an essential network of support for him and his brother, something he said he never forgot in his later years.

Charlie, now 53, was not well-equipped to raise two boys by himself. Sadly, he soon lost his self-sufficiency, for alcohol demanded to be the center of his life. Grandmother Rebecca stepped in to help raise her grandsons at this critical time. As a widow of 30 years by then, she had already experienced the death of two of her five grown children (one who had been shot by a jealous young man when he showed interest in the man's girlfriend, and one who died at age 50 of unknown causes). Grandmother Rebecca was made of "stern stuff," as my dad used to say. She knew what was needed.

They remained living at the Ranch House, as it served as an important anchor. I could see how Grandmother Rebecca had offered what two boys badly needed: care and love. She had instilled a much-

needed stability to her grandsons' lives. In his later years, Dad shared
he had always valued the basics she taught him. "She taught us how
to take care of ourselves, how to do our own laundry and how to
cook," he had said with a deeply-felt indebtedness.

The Ranch House today.

Anything that led to being self-sufficient was highly regarded
by my dad. Grandmother Rebecca became one of his first teachers
in this way. In his later years, as tears filled his eyes, he had said,
"Never did a day go by that I did not appreciate her effort to teach
me these essential skills as a boy. It meant everything to me."

He continued to reflect on his past, to reveal that Uncle
Sim had been another positive force. "Uncle Sim was a constant
presence in our lives, especially as we became teenaged boys.
He showed us how to be successful in life. He took us aside on
more than one occasion when we were getting into mischief, as

boys frequently did. He showed us a better way to behave. He was stern, yet caring. He did what any loving relative would do. There was never a day that went by that we didn't thank him for his love and guidance. He became our strong father figure besides a highly respected mentor."

Sadly, it had become obvious that Charlie was neither. Even though he worked sporadically as a farm manager, as soon as the crops were in, he disappeared. Dad said he went on "benders." These lasted for weeks or even months at a time. No one really knew where he went or when he would return home.

"When he did return home, it was never good," Dad had revealed one day as we spoke about this part of his past. He went on to say he and his brother had known drinking only served to fan the flames of Charlie's uncontrollable rage. "When our dad returned home from being on a bender, we lived in dread. He always looked haggard, completely disheveled. He was so mean." He directed this seething ferocity at his sons: "Even though I don't know what you two boys have been up to, you've probably gotten into some kind of trouble while I was away. That deserves a whippin'!" I take a moment to ask Charlie in spirit about this. *My rage was ignited by a past hidden from view. My failings were piling up, shame engulfed me. Disappointment never left me alone. I couldn't find my way.*

During the times Charlie was around, the beatings were every Sunday in the woodshed. He truly believed this weekly ritual served as a deterrent to any bad behavior in the future. When Sunday arrived, Dad said they were in agony. Looking for anything that would distract him never worked. Their own rage grew with every beating. In time, however, as Dad and Herb got older, grew taller and became stronger, they joined forces, finally bringing an end to these beatings one Sunday, by facing him head-on. Their newly acquired 16- and 17-year-old adult voices bore a new conviction as they forcefully said: "If you don't stop whippin' us, we're going to whip you until you can't get up!" (At that point, the brothers had also become skilled boxers in their own right, having followed in the footsteps of their half-brother, a man who had been a professional boxer until, sadly, he went to prison for fixing fights.) They meant every word. In that moment of confrontation, Charlie knew he could no longer get away with behaving in this way and backed down in the face of his sons' united power. The beatings stopped. However, my dad said any modicum of respect they had for him was now long gone.

I had only heard fragments of this story over time from my Culley cousins, and did not hear this full account until Dad became sober, and was doing the work of connecting this part of his past to the present. Once he had finished sharing this devastating account, my initial shock turned to horror as the gruesome scene became vivid. By today's standards, this behavior would be considered child abuse. Despite what might have been accepted behavior at the time, I wondered how anyone could behave this way. This was Dad's father. And... my grandfather. This realization enraged me. I wanted to disown Charlie, and permanently remove his name from our family tree. Coming to terms with having a grandparent who behaved like this toward people I loved was a struggle that took some time for me to understand.

The disease of alcoholism had prevented few of Charlie's positive qualities from being seen, in fact obscuring any positive qualities altogether and rendering him to appear worthless in every way. It took many years before I realized how beaten down Charlie really had been. I felt sad for everyone involved, both the abused and the abusers. In recalling what Dad had said about his mother's drinking, "Nothing good ever comes from it," over time my anger transformed to sadness in recognition of how his father's legacy later repeated in Dad's own life.

Alta's life had predictable challenges for Dad's sisters. For his oldest sister, Muriel, marriage would come early, just as it had in her mother's life. At the age of 15 with Alta being one of the witnesses, Muriel married a young man five years her senior who came from a family well established in the area. (According to Muriel's two children, their dad's side of the family was a central guiding force for them growing up.)

I wondered if Alta had been happy for Muriel's marriage—one that promised a new start to life—or had she been secretly relieved she no longer had financial or parental responsibility for her oldest child (one of my dad's greatest concerns)? Would she have had enough insight to guide Muriel as such a young bride to make her path a bit easier? No matter what, it looked like a large part of the past could repeat itself. From spirit, Alta now shares: *"I wanted something better for Muriel. The only way I saw that happening was through marriage. Being next to her on her wedding day was a happy event for me. She had a new beginning. I couldn't see beyond that."*

Lila, the youngest in the family, now found herself subject to her mother's behavior minus the buffer of protection from her older sister. The two eventually made their way back to settle in central Oregon. Alta resumed working as a waitress as the Depression persisted, while Lila attended school. Six years later, Alta re-married, this time to Charlie's cousin. Some of my Culley cousins used to say Alta joked by saying that at least she kept it all in the family ensuring she did not have to change her last name this time! This story was one of the few things I knew about Alta. I did not find it very flattering. Rather than finding it funny, I found it quite sad.

I ask Alta to share her views now. *"Marriage provided stability. I always thought it would bring me love, too."* She shows me how sad her heart was at the time; tears fall from it, the image a poignant depiction of a longing to be taken care of, to be nurtured and cherished, that was never met.

Sadly, within four years, she found marriage to Charlie's cousin impossible, even harder than her first marriage had been. He, too, was abusive. Furthermore, alcohol was there once more to worsen the situation.

Lila witnessed her mother's escalating chaotic behavior compounded by her chronic instability. According to Lila's two children, Lila had been happy to leave when she married at age 19. Due to her mother's alcoholic behavior, within subsequent serial marriages, Lila's memories were a string of painful events from which she wanted to distance.

The devastating effects of the Depression were still prevalent everywhere. Weston, where Dad and Herb continued to live, had long been known as a leading brick-making and milling center, and this was reflected in the unique character of many of the commercial buildings—some still standing today—made from bricks supplied by several brick-making companies. Sadly, these brickworks closed in the early 1930s. The only bank was shuttered. The sole hotel, along with several other brick buildings, was torn down after being taken over by another company for back taxes owed. Even though Weston was well-known for its profitable dry land wheat farms in addition to successful crops of green peas (often advertised as "the green pea capital of the world"), Depression agriculture prices made farming a very risky business. It was not much different anywhere else, either. Survival by *any means possible* was the new normal.

Getting a fuller picture of Dad's history helped me comprehend how his early trauma originated. It also helped me understand my undefined feeling, as a sensitive child, of what I had felt lurked in the shadows of my family, unspoken, not to be disturbed, for many years. Like a sponge, I had absorbed remnants of his sadness, his unexpressed anger, and later, his despair. I saw how adverse circumstances became the force behind his desire to create something better for himself. Now, I appreciated why he repeatedly said, "There's no need to dig up the past, honey, nothing good comes from it." Even though I did not agree with his philosophy, it now clarified why I never knew his parents' history (or grandparents' story), or even their first names, until I was well into adulthood.

Here was the link between unhealed emotional pain next to alcoholism, between abuse and serial marriages, and a fragmented family life path leading to depression. Pain begets pain. I saw the need to use secrecy over the past as a means to numb the haunting pain. While denial is time-limited, and can only keep the pain of the past at bay for so long, its firm grip had allowed the façade of my happy well-adjusted family to be intact. Yet any hint of the impact of unaddressed trauma—both on those initially exposed to it and those who inherited it—had been buried.

Chapter 3

Hopes and Dreams

The town of Weston became the "village" my dad and Herb needed. Grandma Rebecca continued to offer a steady presence, and Uncle Sim provided his well-respected leadership. My dad said he had also found support from an older couple living in town (whose names I have sadly forgotten). Treating him like a son, they provided a safe, loving retreat whenever he needed it, easily offering their guidance. He later revealed that their loving presence gave him the critical hand up he had needed as a boy.

I could now draw the thread through his formative years of the effects from his parents' divorce, their addiction to alcohol, and the profound effect of the Depression. I also recognized how adversity became a powerful teacher. In his later years, despite these past perils, he reflected on how he had learned some of his greatest lessons, simply and succinctly stating, "I learned the value of applying myself in everything I did. I set goals for myself. I excelled as best I could. I knew my effort would pay off one day."

Having to work long hours to help bring in the crops late summer through early fall, my dad always knew he did not want to be a farmer. The backbreaking work of throwing bales of hay onto the back of moving flatbed trucks in the intense August heat took strength and stamina. Noting while it had been a way to earn money for the time being, he definitely saw more for himself.

He had a dream: to finish high school while aiming for college. This was a tall order, since few people had the necessary resources at the time. It took money, ambition, and the confidence to risk leaving familiar surroundings in search of something greater. Never a question, he said he was ALL IN no matter what it might require.

He was used to working long hours. Also, he valued working with others. Participating in sports gave him a much-needed outlet for his pent-up energy and frustration. He enjoyed the camaraderie he found on the high school basketball team. He also found a great sense of accomplishment as the catcher on the school's baseball squad (something he would continue to participate in as a college student).

Admittedly, there was just one thing my dad could not control or avoid: Charlie's public displays of drunkenness. "We never knew when this would happen," he told me one day when we were discussing the perils of addiction once he had been committed to sobriety, "however, when it did, it was mortifying." This memory that had remained hidden for many years had surfaced: "One day while Herb and I were in high school, we heard a ruckus outside on the school playground. We all ran over to look out of the long sash windows that lined that side of the classroom. As we I looked out, we saw our father yelling obscenities to anyone who would listen. His speech was obviously impaired. His arms were flailing wildly about as he tried to maintain balance. He shouted obscenities to anyone and everyone. He was obviously drunk."

In the recounting, Dad's emotions were raw, barely filtered. Disgust filled his tone. He finished the story by saying, "Now the whole school knew about our father's drunkenness. Herb and I were unspeakably humiliated."

Again, I felt the embarrassment Dad carried from the past. These episodes were etched in my mind and on my heart. It made the ugliness of alcoholism abundantly clear: an affliction that had torn his family apart and silenced them to live in secrecy.

Dad said that day had sealed his future, inspiring even more determination to focus on what he could control. He defined his plan; he worked his plan. He remained true to his goal: he was leaving. He was college-bound.

He also took a stand on alcoholism. Yes, both of his parents were alcoholics, as I read in an entry from his World War II diary years later. He convinced himself through sheer determination not to follow in their shoes. He would sidestep this curse, having witnessed its devastation firsthand. Knowing this, and applying will power, became the elements of his formula. He (naïvely) believed it would guarantee his immunity.

Returning to the familiar box of old photos and memorabilia, I found his high school graduation announcement, from the spring of 1936. It listed him along with his 10 (yes, just 10) classmates as graduates of Weston Union High School. They had selected their class motto to be: *"Always lead, never follow."* A very fitting statement that clearly defined my dad, as I later knew him.

Alongside his plan and determination, having enough money was critical. He soon realized he did not have enough to begin his first year. Disappointed, he delayed entry for a year, staying in Weston to work in farming and other related businesses. The industry of farming was changing, no longer using teams of horses to pull combines to harvest the wheat. Now they used gasoline operated tractors. No matter how you looked at it though, it was still hard work. I remember him talking about this time in his life once I was out of college. Now from spirit, he says: *"This was a test for me. I had to rise to the occasion to make it happen. It was hard. It gave me a challenge to rise to. And I liked that."*

His recollections also revealed how that time of work gave him additional time to garner hope in order to hone his dream. He had set his sights on attending Oregon State College (later to become Oregon State University) located in Corvallis, over 300 miles away from Weston. OSC specialized in the study of agriculture, something he knew quite a bit about. His pursuit of a degree in plant and crop science would one day place him at the center of the lucrative fast-growing agri-business industry.

I now ask him in spirit what it was like for him as he entered his freshman year in 1938. *"A very demanding time for me. I was terribly unprepared for the rigors of college-level work. Few people from my high school went to college. Teachers weren't accustomed to preparing their students for this."* "Were you scared or overwhelmed by what you faced?" I ask. *"I was scrambling. I knew I had to perform. I had to scramble to seek out what I needed in order to succeed."* As he describes this, his energy is frenetic. *"I was used to being a big frog in a little pond."* He's referring not only to the change in size of the town he came from but the contrast in school size; both were exponentially greater. *"I studied night and day. I joined a fraternity of like-minded men. They helped show me the way."* Several mementos remain of Dad's college years in the photo box, including his fraternity pin, as well as a picture of him seated next to his fraternity brothers on the front lawn outside of their house. He sits in the first row wearing a casual dark sports jacket, a style fitting of the late 1930s, light-collared shirt, light-colored pants, dress socks and shoes. He looks straight at the camera, arms folded across his lap, showing a relaxed, confident posture. The air is one of belonging.

Despite being an uphill battle, my dad succeeded in passing his first-year courses. However, his studies were soon interrupted, once again, due to the lack of required funds. "Poppy, I would have been so discouraged to experience this! How did you cope?" *"I did what I had to do. I needed more money. There was no point in being undone by this. I pushed away any feelings that threatened my success. I returned to Weston, lived at the Ranch House, working as much as I could."* "How much was alcohol in your life at this time?" I ask, wondering how he seemed to successfully push his emotions to the side (a tendency that often fuels addiction). *"When not working I spent what time I could among friends still in the area. We always drank, never thinking much of it. It was a release for me. The effects didn't impact me or the direction I was headed, so all was good."*

One of the things which always stood out for me was seeing his tenacity and drive even at an early age. When he had a singular focus, he never wavered. He was ALL IN no matter what might seem to interfere. Now I could see where this approach had begun.

Once having gathered enough money to finish college, (aided by some financial help from Herb as well as Charlie; yes, Charlie somehow had come through, at times), he returned to school, setting his sights both on his academics along with joining an Oratory Club on campus to hone critical thinking and speaking skills. He had come a long way from his early childhood years of having a noticeable speech impediment that made it difficult to pronounce the letters "L" and "S" (something that had plagued me as well as a child). It did not help that his half-sister and sister both had first names beginning with L. He used to tell me how his speech impairment made him the target of teasing. However he was not teased by his grade school classmates for long before he said his brother took him aside, showing him where in his mouth to position his tongue for each L and S-sounding word to correct the pronunciation. I was amazed when I learned this. Not only that he had overcome this, but by how observant his brother had been to know what to do. From a very unlikely start, he found what would become a life-long passion: public speaking.

Capturing first prize in the men's division when the Oratory Club entered the "State Old Line" contest in 1940/1941 was the result of his passion. "Poppy, I discovered the typed copy of your speech in some of your things after you died, the one that brought you the first-place honor. (The topic was about increasing community awareness regarding syphilis; it was personal to him since a relative had recently died of the disease.) Why did you keep it all those years?" *"I had a wonderful mentor who was the advisor to the club. He guided me. He encouraged me to excel. He saw something in me worth nurturing. I was deeply grateful. I also liked competition. I liked to push myself to see how far I could get. Keeping it reminded me of this crucial time in my life; it defined me in a new way."*

His hard work paired with his intense desire to succeed had paid off. He had come a long way as a boy from a small farming town in northeastern Oregon, enduring the effects of the Depression, divorced parents, a fragmented family, and alcoholism. Yet it was December of 1941. The American fleet in Pearl Harbor, Hawai'i had just been bombed by the Japanese. In a matter of days, the country was at war on two fronts: one with Japan, the other with Nazi Germany. Graduation, just six months away, would sadly have to be postponed.

Inside of three weeks of this act of war, Dad said he had dropped out of college, immediately enlisting in the military. As was true for many Americans at the time, he was willing to do whatever was needed for his country. Plus he was eager to prove himself. He joined the Army Air Corps (later to become the Air Force) being sent to Ft Lewis, Washington to await orders.

His diary covering the war years was also among the contents of the box of photos I was going through to uncover more of his past. The finely-woven navy fabric covering the small pocket-sized book was worn in places, although the brass clasp and lock were still remarkably intact. A thin maroon ribbon marked the place of his first entry where he wrote:

"My first diary. A period of war and turbulence demands of me that I keep some record (personal thoughts) of events taking place during this historical era."

His next entry gave me a flavor of his life at the time:

"We were granted five hours leave today and I went to Tacoma for the second time in my life. It was really nice to see civilians rushing around shopping for Christmas, after our being shut in due to war threats on the Pacific coast. These have subsided somewhat, but the boys on P.I., Hawai'i, Guam, and those islands are seeing lots of action with Japan."

I gathered insights as to what mattered most to him in his comment about some of the men he was around:

"These are good, simple, basically sound fellows-all seemingly with a rare sense of humor."

Yet, when Christmas Day arrived, I sadly began to see alcohol becoming more central to his life. He wrote:

"Celebrated with several beers in our wigwam and a swell feast."

The next day:

"More beer, celebration, and drinking for three hours steady."

A few days later:

"Went to town and proceeded on what resulted in a near tragic binge; I was late to camp and the wrath of those in power descended on me. All passes were canceled and I'm doing a week of pearl diving (peeling potatoes). Hope this blows over."

And finally:

"Just when making progress for Brigadier Headquarters staff, I pulled this (being drunk)-will have hard time regaining ground. This is a turning point for me concerning drinking."

I took some very deep breaths after reading these entries. I was shocked to see that rarely did a day go by when he did not have an entry about his drinking. A few years before, he had promised himself drinking would not be central to his life. Now it was. The early signs of trouble were blatantly there.

One day later, on New Year's Eve, the only thing he wrote was:

"Gaiety is lacking here except that coming from bottles."

I am sure gaiety was lacking for everyone on the eve of war with Japan. It was undeniably a time of great uncertainty…it must have been terrifying. To Dad's credit, he had survived his childhood years of abuse and neglect, overcoming many obstacles along the way. He also had experienced support from his "village," next to excelling in college. The one thing he had not bargained on, however, was the mounting emotional costs due to his troubled past. I think these buried long forgotten feelings now slowly began to fuel his compulsive pull towards alcohol. I ask Poppy for his perspective from spirit. *"I had no clue anything bad was happening. It crept up on me, never registering as a problem. I couldn't let myself see it that way. I had overcome many things. I thought I was handling it just fine."*

Years later in his life, once Dad was sober, he told me just how much he liked both the taste and euphoria achieved when he drank. He said it erased all evidence of trauma. He could move forward beyond these complications. I have always wondered if this pull began even earlier, perhaps in high school, despite his firm resolution not to let alcohol control his life. Maybe he did not see having a few too many beers at a weekend party as the beginning of a destructive pattern. That was, and still is, a common misconception.

Yet, his lack of understanding only served to make his story classic. The struggle to deploy different strategies to control his drinking intake, by modifying it or cutting it back, is known to be one of the most universal hallmarks leading to alcoholic behavior.

He was clueless. So were a lot of people at the time. Fear had enveloped everyone in the country in its terrifying grip. Alcohol provided an easy opportunity for escape. The simple truth was alcohol made most people feel better. At least for a while.

From the late 1940s illustrating a prevailing attitude about alcohol use.

Chapter 4

Unparalleled Success

The war was on. Our country rallied, creating a unified focus: to do whatever necessary to win the battles being fought, both in Europe and the Pacific. The five years that my dad served in the military brought him relentless challenges, followed by many hard-earned accomplishments he seldom spoke of until later.

"Never did I realize that my greatest challenges would be of a personal nature," he reflected one day as we were talking about this later in his life. Logic always told him to focus only on the tasks at hand. His major strategy was mind over matter. His first diary entry for January 1, 1942 questions the effectiveness of his resolve, however.

"A new year tumbling after the old sans fanfare here in the woods. Resolutions: No asinine drinking and save at least 1/3 of pay."

Once again, he wrote about the past effects of his drinking. I wondered what had led to his declaration of "no more asinine drinking."

Something must have happened to require such a clear resolution. As my dad, he tended to leave out information crucial to understanding certain events. In other words, he rarely told the WHOLE story; only what he wanted to hear; what he wanted others to know. As a child, I usually noticed when something critical was not being said; it always left me confused. As a teenager, I became both a keen observer of what was not being said, as well as someone who filled in those blanks by blurting out what I thought had been left out; usually, I was right.

The diary entry six months later told of his experience during flight training in Santa Ana, CA:

"The pressure was grueling. Pilots were 'washing out' every week."

He felt very lucky not to be one of them. Despite having ended up in the hospital for two weeks, suffering from a severe bronchial infection, having to double his efforts to catch up to his flight class, he completed primary followed by advanced training after an intense year-and-a-half of work. Anyone who has gone through military flight training knows how demanding it can be.

Several months after relocating to Santa Ana, he met my mom, Gladys (Glad) McCullough. She had previously moved from Illinois to California accompanied by one of her sisters, and had found work at the Glendale Airport. Between trainings and relocations, they forged their relationship. They surprised everyone when they decided to marry in the spring of 1943. It came as a surprise to many because Mom never showed the least bit of interest in becoming serious with any of her numerous suitors. Prior to moving to Los Angeles, she had worked for a newspaper in Champaign, Illinois, writing a weekly column. She even had the honor of interviewing Eleanor Roosevelt (wife of President Franklin Roosevelt) during her visit to Mom's home town. (I only learned this from her younger sister when I discovered a picture of Mom next to Mrs. Roosevelt; she never wanted to talk about it, saying it was no big deal—she, too, had her secrets.) She was used to being independent. She was used to city ways. She was sophisticated, along with dressing beautifully. Dad said he had been captivated. In addition, she defied convention at the time by being seriously attracted to a man, my dad, nine years her junior (a fact I only found out after her death years later).

For my dad, Mom was unlike any woman he had ever dated. He revealed his deeper feelings about her (which surprised me to know) in his diary a year after they married:

"Ours wasn't the usual courtship—probably the most unconventional. Glad didn't arouse any sensual lust—she isn't too attractive physically. It is her inherent make-up, a knowing personality, a rare psychologist, but I don't believe she is aware of that point; clear-thinking and straightforward with a charm unsurpassed by any other girl I've ever known. Not at all wifey nor domestic. I knew our life would never run along a settling-down process to raise a family. Here is what I had always wanted in a woman and at long last it appeared. I've never known what Glad's feelings were for sure before we were married except that she professed to love me and I was so moved I could hardly believe the impossible to be true."

On April 12th, 1943, alongside a few friends in attendance, my parents married in Stockton, California. In the picture taken that day as they left the church, Mom was wearing what Dad had requested: An emerald green suit, the knee-length hemline trimmed in fur, a stylish matching hat along with matching shoes. He was in full military dress looking quite confident and happy. Shortly after they married, my dad wrote in his diary:

"Commissioned with wings. Married Glad. Hugest day in my life. Left for five-day honeymoon to L.A. Sweetest girl in the world."

My parents' wedding day April 1943.

To top it off, the same day he got his wings and married, OSC granted him (in absentia) his B.S. degree in crop science. Even though Dad was six months away from graduating when he enlisted, the college honored his, and others', commitment to fighting the war by awarding his degree early. After all of his hard work to complete college, I could only imagine what a gift this had been to him at the time. This dream he had worked so hard to realize was finally achieved. I could definitely see how this was the *hugest* day in his life.

By the fall, with all of his training completed, he received orders for the Central Pacific.

As the eve of combat approached, he was acutely aware of the character of the men around him. At one point, he wrote about a fellow officer who was losing his nerve, nurturing his dislikes, his shortcomings as well as using liquor to ease him along. Dad questioned whether he would be someone he could depend on in a life or death situation. He did not respect anyone who could not be all in when it came to being a member of his team.

Yet, he realized that it would be inevitable for some men to die. As he pondered the possibility he might be one of them, he wrote:

"As I look forward to the possibility of dying I can feel few misgivings. Perhaps it is because I cannot feel deeply enough. At any rate if such happens to me I will feel its inevitability knowing myself that my life hasn't been an empty one, but one filled with all the emotions and deep feelings that any person can possess. The paramount issue in my 25 years was my marriage to Gladys McCullough. I'll never know how such a merger came to pass. As far as material accomplishments are concerned—I am a failure. But if living a happy, full, complete life, living every moment is the yardstick to success, then I belong to that category."

I am struck by how articulate he had been about what was most important to him. Years later, at one of the lowest points in his life, he would be guided to rediscover this important philosophy about success: living every moment of life being happy, full, and complete.

By the spring of 1944, advancing from crew member to copilot, in addition to proving himself able and worthy, he finally got his own plane and crew. He proudly named his B-25 bomber "The Beachcomber." In one of several pictures, he, together with his five crew members, all dressed in their flight suits, stands in front of their plane, looking seasoned and confident. To the left of the plane's window in large stenciled letters reads: LT. C.S. Culley. Next to his name are slash marks indicating how many successful bombing missions he had flown to that point: 22.

Dad (back row, left) with flight crew. Now 22 missions flown.

As a young child, I used to look through all of the war pictures kept in the bottom drawer of my parents' dresser. I sat on the floor of their bedroom, in front of the open drawer, going through one picture after another. I was fascinated by the various aerial shots taken from Poppy's plane during raids while stationed on one of several islands in the South Pacific. At the time, I had no idea what they meant. Now, as I look at each picture, fragments of this time in his life unfold. The smaller-sized pictures were of the native people on whose islands he and his squadron were stationed. Another series of pictures were of Bob Hope next to the many who accompanied him to entertain the troops. Numerous other photos were of fellow pilots and crew members ready to fly a combat mission, or of them all proudly guzzling bottles of alcohol in one hand, while holding the next round in the other. The one that touched my heart most was a picture of him sitting at his makeshift wooden desk in his tent, smoking his pipe while gazing at a picture of Mom. He looked in love.

While many of the black and white photos showed people smiling, laughing, drinking or proudly preparing to fly, Dad later said never did a day go by when he didn't wonder who would not return from their mission that day. Finally, by the time he flew his 50th and final mission in September 1944, he wrote in his diary:

"Good raid over the island of Nauru. Medium Altitude. ALL DONE. THANK GOD."

For his combat service, he received several medals, among them the Distinguished Flying Cross. He rarely spoke of them, only saying many people were recognized in this way while many people died as a result of their service. He kept silent about the horrific things he had witnessed in combat until many years later. At the time, it was not customary to boast or dwell on one's accomplishments during the war. To him, it was a team effort, pure and simple.

Once stateside, he happily joined Mom while completing the rest of his service obligation in Colorado Springs, Colorado. He resumed flight training, resulting in more accomplishments, becoming licensed as a commercial pilot with a multi-engine rating. He also received the highly-coveted green card signifying achievement of master status as a pilot. When he was promoted to captain in August 1945, the war had finally ended. Despite his many accomplishments, he was only too happy to be discharged from the military five months later, saying (as he had about farming), it was not a way of life for him.

My parents returned to Southern California where they had close friends. For the time being, Mom's two sisters also lived nearby. Housing was not easy to find at the time. Somehow they managed. My dad held his hard-earned college degree in hand, set on finding work in agricultural sales. A year later (on the very day I was born), he received his dream job offer and accepted a position at a large, well-established chemical company which focused on agri-business and chemical sales. I am sure I could use his previous expression to describe another *"hugest day"* in his life.

Like many families at that time, my parents were eager to create a new life, no longer subject to the entanglements brought on by war. Finding stable profitable employment, next to owning a car and a home became their goals. Despite his diary entry during the war saying he did not think he and Mom would have a lifestyle conducive to raising a family, their priorities obviously changed.

Dottie and Wickie, my parents' closest friends and my beloved godparents, used to talk about the day I was born, feeling great joy (always endearing for me to hear).

"We never laughed so hard as when we realized we got to the hospital long before your mom and dad! We were so excited about this day." Mom added a different perspective to the story by saying, "Yes, when you were born, your father immediately fainted in the waiting room. All of the nurses were so worried about him that they rushed over to take care of him, completely forgetting about me." (Being forgotten or being in the background of Dad's life was to become a theme later in their relationship, especially when alcohol abuse was involved.)

Me as an infant with dad. 1947.

Sitting on a blanket on the lawn at our rental house in West Covina, CA.
Mom (left), me, godmother Dottie, and cousin Penny.

I bonded immediately with my dad. I was crazy about him.
I liked how he greeted me, held me, included me, and let me help
with projects. I was constantly by his side when he was home. The
only thing I did not like: his constant smoking. Also Mom's, too. I
could not stand how the house smelled, or how my clothes and hair
reeked of cigarette smoke. A lot of people smoked in the 1950s: in
their cars, restaurants, and movie theaters. Mom even smoked while
she got her hair done in the beauty shop every week.

By the time I was three, my parents bought their first home for $10,000 (imagine that today!). It meant more room, a nice neighborhood plus other children my age. Dad's job was to sell fertilizers and chemicals to vendors who serviced the agricultural needs of Southern California, a role he used to teasingly refer to as a "manure peddler!" At the time, much of the fertile land in Southern California was ideal for growing a wide variety of fruits and vegetables. Having a large territory to service, with air travel not being an option at the time, he drove from vendor to vendor, leaving home every Monday morning then returning every Friday night.

Dad's schedule meant Mom and I were home alone during the week. In some ways, she was an enigma to me. I knew she cared about me. She looked for activities I might be interested in, like dance classes or swimming lessons. She let me play music on their record player while in my bedroom. On the inside, however, she seemed unhappy. I could sense by her level of upset by the way she approached ironing the weekly basket of clothes each week. If she forcefully tried to get every wrinkle out of the shirt or blouse draped over the wall-mounted ironing board, I knew she was unhappy. I tried to find ways to be helpful at those moments. Often nothing helped. Minus any other options, I resigned myself to go outside to play ball with my dog, Cindy.

In the backyard of our home in Whittier, CA, with dog Cindy. Hair in pin curls and unhappy about having my picture taken.

Cindy was the best. But no matter how much fun we had playing, I still felt a lingering sadness for Mom. (Later in her life she revealed she was more comfortable around children once they were more independent and verbal. Knowing this made me realize how trapped she must have felt…coupled with the bind I was caught in, as well.) Even at my young age, I figured out how to stay inside "the box" of acceptable behavior; I knew what would keep things calm. It meant little permission for curiosity, spontaneity, or misbehaving.

Yet, sometimes, I could not help myself. I rebelled whenever Mom wanted to take a picture of me. She always wanted me to look good. She made sure I had a permanent wave in my hair (not my choice), styled my hair the way she liked, and dressed me in clothes she preferred. As I stood before the camera, I made sure I had a scowl on my face. Or, I looked away. I did not want to please her or conform to her wishes. I just wanted to be left alone. Sometimes I would even deliberately scuff the toes of the new shoes she bought me, if I did not like them. She always chose shoes that were good for my feet, even though they were rarely worn by other kids. It caused me to stand out, and feel out of place among my classmates (never a good thing). Underneath, I knew I was not what she had expected as a daughter. Years later, I realized I had understood that in order to fulfill her ideal, I would have to give up too much of myself. Even at a young age, I had somehow known I could not do that. I carried a stubborn streak, fed by pent-up anger, any time she wanted to define me. I now ask her to share her thoughts now from spirit. *"We were alike in many ways. I, too, rebelled in my family. I wanted to discover my own path, but had a very controlling father who thought otherwise. You were determined. And so was I. It put us at odds."* I am surprised to hear this from Mom, realizing for the first time how alike we were.

Once home, Dad was only too happy to stay home, giving Mom the time she needed for herself. Once she was out for the day, Dad and I worked on projects together, in the house, garage, or garden. One day, we decided to plant pansies underneath the two orange trees we had in our back yard. Once we bought the flowers, we got busy preparing the soil, planting, fertilizing each plant, followed by watering everything. I loved how it looked; the faces on the pansies always looked so happy. We could work contentedly like this for hours.

In many ways, it was a *sweet time* for me on the outside. On the inside, it was troubling. I could feel an undercurrent of unexpressed emotion on any given day. It could be about Dad (probably about his family, work, or Mom) or about Mom (likely about her troublesome oldest sister or her lack of freedom now that I was on the scene, or Dad). Whatever the reasons, it made me vigilant, always scanning for turbulence. The only thing I knew to do when I sensed a disturbance was to find a way to please either or both of my parents. It seemed to work most of the time. I learned to calm the waters by helping Mom in the kitchen or doing housework, sitting by Dad while he read, or being on my best behavior while at the dinner table. The times when this did not work, I would take Cindy outside, play music in my room, or find a neighbor-friend to ride bikes with. No matter what I did to distract myself though, I always felt an uneasy emotional disturbance. I had no one to talk to about it. Even if I had, what would I have said? Words escaped me. In short order, loneliness found fertile soil in my world. For years, it rarely released me from its bondage.

My dad loved his job at the company he worked for. He was mentored by some of the best in the business. As he became more successful, my parents began to entertain more at our home. Mom was a definite asset. She was a wonderful cook. She knew how to entertain others, easily engaging in witty conversation among a variety of people.

Dad going from town to town selling agricultural supplies (fertilizer and pesticides) to local vendors in the Imperial Valley of CA.

Eventually, their entertaining involved alcohol. Mom had always been a moderate drinker. Dad, knowing his tendency to compulsively drink at times, developed rules around drinking. First, it was a drink every once in a while, then it extended to weekends only allowing one drink before dinner as the limit. The same rule was made clear, as well, to those they entertained. I consult Poppy in spirit. "How did you think this could possibly help you?" Not hesitating he said, *"It seemed logical and simple to me: controlling my drinking meant alcohol wouldn't become a problem."* "Did you really think you could impose these rules on others successfully?" *"I did, at the time. Rules always gave my life order. I had little insight then."*

I was never aware of these rules as a child, only learning about them later from Mom. I remember seeing various bottles of alcohol in the kitchen next to the beautiful glasses used for each type of drink. I also noticed people seemed to be happier and more carefree when they drank.

Dad left outside sales through a promotion to a position within the company that meant he was home every night. That was a welcome relief. His promotion brought a pay raise, which afforded my family a move to a different home in a new nearby neighborhood. Like many families, we were acquiring more material things. It was the 1950s, after all: a culture defined by the acquisition of many time-saving devices like Hoover vacuums and Kelvinator refrigerators.

Some professions, like Dad's, were being defined by the two-martini lunch. Entertaining prospective clients at lunch became a necessary activity which included my dad's participation, along with other executives in the company. He was rising to the top. And he knew it. He was only too happy to do what was expected of him in order to excel. The rule of only one drink before dinner on weekends lost favor to the allure of making another sale.

He was also beginning to excel at golf. He learned to play golf to ease his symptoms of what used to be referred to as "battle fatigue," now known as PTSD, acquired during his combat experiences. At the time, Dad said the Army normalized these symptoms, saying it was due to being in a high-stress, life-or-death situation for a period of time. Once the threat no longer existed, the body and the mind were not able to adjust to less stress. (Notice the lack of awareness about the emotional toll that the horrors of war created.) The remedy was to put everyone in a structured learning environment. In so doing, he re-learned algebra, among several other subjects, and was introduced to the game of golf.

Golf was the perfect game for him. It required great mental concentration along with physical prowess. He loved the inner competition as well as competing against others. More and more business was being conducted on the golf course, especially at what was known as the "19th hole," when everyone retired to the clubhouse for a drink once done playing. He liked the camaraderie of his foursome, he liked re-living his best shots, and telling jokes about what happened during play, as well as being seen as an accomplished golfer. Yet, as time went by, the combined elements of what it took for him to be in top form, constantly numbing himself from the troubling past emotional trauma began to contribute to what would later create a perfect storm for him.

Meanwhile, our family looked forward to taking yearly vacations to the High Sierra Mountains. I loved camping; it was there I learned to ride horses. Every summer we returned to Lake Gregory, my parents to fish, and me to ride my favorite horse, Silver, through the woods for the day. Being in nature was a definite favorite for all of us. Most nights we would cook the trout my parents caught, followed by a trip to the nearby café for my favorite dessert—cherry pie topped with a big scoop of vanilla ice cream. Life seemed less complicated when we were camping. Somehow it was easier to be happy.

By the time I was eight, however, I began to distance myself from the confusing emotional waters present in my family. I no longer asked about things that did not make sense to me, like why when I came home from a wonderful weekend stay at my godparents' home, my dog Cindy was no longer there. "What happened to Cindy?" I had asked, panic growing in my voice as I searched frantically for her in the backyard and in the house. After a lengthy silence, my dad said, "We gave her to a farm family; she needed to be in the country." Later Mom added, "The neighbor kids teased her by poking sticks through the fence; she was always barking at them." That was that. Nothing more would be said. I was heartbroken. I never got to say goodbye. I knew I had to keep my anger and sadness to myself. If I did not, I knew I would get a stern, scolding look from my parents. Harmony would be restored if I gave up my protest. Despite my feelings, I did just that.

When Penny, my older McCullough cousin, came to live at our home as a teenager, I never really knew why. Even though she had been in my life intermittently since I was born, she had never lived with us until now.

Me with Penny having an afternoon tea party.

I had always liked Penny. She was like an older sister. I appreciated her including me in her activities when she could. We were both only children, grateful for the friendships we found at school. I was used to seeing pictures of her together with Mom before I was born, even before my parents had met. I knew Mom had tried to help Penny's mom (Mom's older sister and a single parent at the time) by taking Penny on weekends. I guessed it was about her mother's tendency to value her love life over my cousin's well-being. However, I was never sure. I just knew it was great to share a bedroom and have some company. I loved looking at her poodle skirts next to her saddle shoes in our shared closet. I also did not know why Mom suddenly had a part-time job. I just knew she brought home typing to do, which I helped with. A few years later, when Penny came home one night with her boyfriend she told my parents they had just eloped. No one could deny that something big had just happened. The momentary shock on my parents' faces revealed their disbelief. After a quick recovery, however, Dad calmly said, "Well, it looks like we have some things to talk about. Let's go to the kitchen to see what your plans are." As the four of them went behind closed doors, I was left alone in the living room. Clearly not being included, I quietly went to my bedroom with Penny's dog, Josie, escaping by reading one of my favorite books. After that night, nothing more was said. But I felt the reverberations for weeks.

When those confusing moments added up over time, making it impossible for me to stay compliant, I provoked Mom; it was my way of acting out about things I did not like or understand. The easiest way to irritate her was to ride my bike around the neighborhood, wearing just shorts (minus a top). My riding topless sent her through the roof! "Pamela," she would yell from the driveway, "get back in here right this minute, and put on a shirt. You know better than to do this!" She was always exasperated. I knew she was embarrassed by me being "immodest" for a girl of nine. In spite of her objections I felt quietly triumphant. I had made her notice me.

School and friends were my priorities, as were my animals. By this time, I had quite a menagerie (possibly due to my parents' guilt about Cindy). I had my parakeet, Skipper, Mr. Hopper, my turtle who used to hibernate for the winter under my bed, and several goldfish. Of course, there was also Penny's dog, who we all enjoyed. Mom rarely had to ask me to feed them or clean their cages or bowls. I happily took good care of them. I would have happily taken care of a horse, too (or so I thought, at the time). However, I knew fantasy would never trump reality in my family. Knowing I would never have a real one, I got imaginative. In my mind, I turned my bike into a make-believe horse. Dad made me a special "stall" where I could park my "horse," feeding it left over grass clippings. When not in school or attending to my animal friends, I could always count on my close friend and neighbor, Cheri, to ride bikes with. Her parents always included me in their family.

A busy outer life allowed me to push away the nagging questions about why things at home were the way they were. The unspoken family rule was feelings had no place in family discussions. I learned to accept what I saw at face value. Looking back, I see how I began to close my heart to my own yearnings and dreams. It had made sense. I had to look out for myself to gain emotional balance; there was little room for anything else.

I happily entered the fifth grade in 1957, not realizing a big change was underfoot. It was late fall when my parents took me aside saying, "Honey, we're moving to Oregon. I've gotten a job transfer. I will soon be working in Portland." At first, I had no idea what this meant, other than I would no longer be at the same school. Then, it sunk in: I would not only change schools, but I would have to say good-bye to my dear friend, Cheri. However, my relationship with Cheri had recently changed in such an unexpected way. A few weeks earlier, when I had gone to her house one day to see if she could play, her mom had not been her usual friendly self. I had been very surprised she was not happy to see me. When I asked if Cheri could ride bikes, she said in an uncharacteristically cool tone, "We've decided Cheri needs to have other friends. It's best you go elsewhere to play." My jaw dropped. I could not fathom what this was about. What did she mean Cheri needed other friends? I knew she had other friends besides me. Now, I no longer had Cheri as a friend. On top of it, I was not welcome in their family either, two big losses I could not understand. Had I done something wrong? Feeling crazy, all I wanted to do was to get out of there. I made a beeline for my bike, and went riding as fast I could, the bright, colorful handlebar streamers whipping in the wind. I relentlessly circled around all of my favorite places in the neighborhood, until the crazy-making feelings were finally spent. Once I went in the house, I told Mom what happened, hoping she could provide some explanation. She barely glanced up from what she was doing when she said, "Yes, that's probably for the best." Reeling from what Mom said, my thoughts collided, one after the other. What is going on here? How could this possibly be for the best? I felt incredibly confused. No one seemed to offer me any comfort or support, or even an explanation. When all was said and done, I felt rejected by Cheri's mom, abandoned by my own, and devastated by the loss of my dear friend.

Years later, after Dad's cancer diagnosis, he confessed he had not been a good husband to Mom (or good father to me). "When we left California years ago, it wasn't just because of the increased congestion, pollution, and my job transfer. It was also because of a possible indiscretion I had." He did not say how far this relationship had gone. He just said the four of them (my parents along with the other couple) had sat down and discussed "the matter," agreeing to part ways. It did not take long before I realized the discretion, or near miss, had probably been with Cheri's mother.

It was winter when we arrived in Portland. I experienced snow for the first time. I had to bundle up in a heavy coat, head scarf, gloves, and boots for the walk to my new school on the southeast side. Even though I was shy being in this new setting, I was grateful to be accepted by the students in Miss Brown's classroom. Life seemed easier, having less traffic and air pollution. There was so much natural beauty around us. Experiencing four distinct seasons was something new to me. Each season brought a variety of recreational activities, whether it be skiing in the winter, picnicking, hiking, camping or fishing in the summer, or visiting one of the many local parks. Our California life was now in the past.

Summer brought the opportunity to visit Dad's brother, Herb, and his family, now only a few hours away. Having remained in Weston after high school, Herb had carried on the tradition of farming. For the first time, I met some of my Culley cousins. They visited us on several occasions. Plus, I spent several weeks at their home in Weston over the course of two summers. My experience of extended family created a whole new world for me.

While working in Portland, Dad got reacquainted with the agricultural needs of Oregon's rich Willamette Valley, located on the west side of the Cascade Mountains, an extension of the Sierra Mountains in California. This fertile valley enabled farmers to grow a large number of crops, most notably various types of grass seed for the rest of the country, and eventually for much of the world.

Over time, Dad began to envision a better way to tailor the way fertilizers and chemicals were distributed to each farmer, based on the individual needs of their soil coupled with the type of crops planted—a dream that would eventually upend my world.

My Portland life revolved around school and friends. Playing the few sports available to girls at the time (long before Title IX was in place), I happily claimed the tomboy in my heart. It did not take long for my initial shyness to give way to feeling anchored and confident in my surroundings through grade school into my first year of high school. Once I had the support I needed from teachers and friends, I excelled. By the end of my freshman year of high school, I had enjoyed being a cheerleader, a member of the Homecoming court, plus meeting my first significant love. I was happily hitting my stride.

Soon came the news that rocked my world. Sitting down with me, a serious no-nonsense look on his face, my dad delivered the blow: "We're leaving Portland and moving to Corvallis (60 miles away). I'm starting my own business in a few weeks. He went on, but I did not hear a thing he said. All I felt was my world coming to an end. I did not want to know anything about Dad's greater ambitions. I was a young teenager, who—finally—had plans of her own.

Even though my parents talked on about the move, I tuned them out. None of it mattered. My world was shattered. Gone were the hopes and budding dreams I had for my next year of high school in Portland. I realized I had no choice. Even though I had to comply (something that was getting harder and harder to do), I slowly found my voice. I unleashed my anger any way I could. I did not care what my parents thought. I yelled my objections, my voice full of contempt: "How can you do this to me? I hate this plan! I'm finally happy." They listened, Mom more than Dad, but nothing changed. Later, as my feelings gained more intensity, I screamed, "What am I supposed to do now?" All I said fell on deaf ears. My parents made the message very clear: we are leaving, end of discussion. Realizing there was no recourse, I cried for days. I moped around, at loose ends in every way. Once my friends learned I was leaving, they gave me a going-away party. It was a bittersweet moment. I still have the bracelet they gave me that day holding a single charm on it that read: "Love from the Gang." Saying goodbye to each of my friends was heartbreaking. By far the most devastating loss for me, though, was saying goodbye to my first serious relationship, my boyfriend of almost a year. Like any 14-year-old, I had not one clue on how to manage this feat.

The overriding focus was the window of opportunity which had now opened for my dad. Having found a business partner willing to invest in his ideas, he was ready to seize the moment in his usual, driven fashion. There was no tolerance for anything that would distract him, namely me and my various forms of rebellion.

In short order, I began my sophomore year in a new high school in a new town. We rented a house until Dad's business could allow for my parents to build a home. My adjustments were big: I had moved from a large four-year high school to a small three-year one. From a large city to a small town. I was not used to the cliques that were in place (some went as far back as grade school), plus the gossip that prevailed. The first week I was in school, I witnessed my first fight between two girls in the dimly-lit lunch cafeteria located in the school's dank, cramped basement. I stared, while they screamed furiously, slapping and punching each other, tearing out large patches of each other's hair. I could not believe my eyes. I had been initiated into a whole new world, devoid of anyone to talk to. I left the cafeteria without lunch, never to return.

I felt out of place for months, completely uprooted. My resentment spewed towards my dad every chance I got, as he moved forward building his business with a singular focus that did not include me. Anything he said to me was met with a subtle snarl or a haughty attitude of indifference.

Before long, he and I were at odds ALL the time. I had not been consulted about this move. I did not care about his dream. I only cared about finding new friends while fitting in at my new high school. But deep down, I felt I was losing my dad.

Gone were the activities that had brought us so close together, among them the many sports he had taught me as I had gotten older. He had been instrumental in teaching me how to play softball, making sure I did not throw the ball "like a girl." Constant practice had helped me later be a good, solid pitcher for my seventh and eighth grade softball team. He had also taught me how to play tennis, badminton, volleyball, and of course, golf. We had played golf a lot. He never wasted an opportunity to instruct me about what I did wrong. Every shot warranted correction. He did the same to Mom. There was no fun here. I longed for him to shut up. A few times, I told him just that. He was always surprised: "Honey, I thought you would want the help. It's the only way you'll excel." He was clueless. He wanted me to have his drive, his passion to compete along with his confidence. I did not have any of it.

As I look back, I wanted him to say he understood the challenges that his dream had created for me. That he knew what it felt like not to have a choice, or a voice, in deciding the course of my life, since he had experienced this very same thing when his parents divorced. Most importantly, I wanted to hear from him we were still a family. A family that would pull together. (I later realized he might have wished for his parents to say the same thing to him and his siblings, as they divorced. Some things were bound to repeat themselves.)

Obviously, driven by his goal, my dad's singular focus meant he was oblivious to anyone else. On one hand, Mom was left to support his dream. On the other hand, she was left to help me manage the rough terrain I now walked. With me being more independent, she was able to be a great help in guiding me through the various social situations I faced at school. She encouraged me to bring friends home. She offered support when I expressed an interest in various activities. She was a good listener when I needed it. Still, she sometimes remained a mystery. Any time I wanted to know more about her past, what her teenaged years had been like, her dating experiences, or what difficult social situations she might have faced, she disappeared behind her large brown eyes with a distant look. Her responses seemed to read from a carefully prepared script, revealing nothing more than what she wanted me to know.

THE GRIP OF
ADDICTION

Chapter 5

The Slippery Slope

I hit my stride by the time I entered my junior year of high school. Mom's guidance and support helped me gain confidence; and being introverted herself, she knew how to handle various social challenges in a way that I could understand. I appreciated how she could be quite perceptive about people. Once again, I had close friends, and was involved in many activities. I even enjoyed dating. Dad happily planned and planted all of the landscape around our new home located in a lovely forested area of town. His business had clearly taken off. My parents had an active social life, being members of the local country club as well as other civic organizations. In Dad's spare time he was also busy establishing himself as an amateur championship golfer.

At school, I looked normal and happy. In contrast, at home, I was moody. It did not help that puberty arrived early for me, even before I was a teenager. Early puberty brought a chronic case of serious acne lasting well into my late 20s. Even though Mom found a dermatologist for me to see on a weekly basis (for which I was so very grateful), I was always embarrassed by how my skin looked. Also, I constantly perspired, ruining many of my blouses. Pinning dress shields into every blouse I wore helped, even though I still felt helplessly self-conscious about everything. Obsessed by insecurity, my inner dialogue revolved around how my hair looked, if I had said and done the right things and if I fit in.

Not only was I moody due to puberty issues, I was moody because of a new shift in my parents' behavior. Sometimes, I noticed how frantic Mom was to get dinner on the table as soon as Dad came home from work. No longer did they enjoy their relaxed "cocktail hour" before dinner, where they would catch up on each other's day. The new routine was to eat immediately before Dad had yet another drink. Mom thought this was a way to slow down the effects of the alcohol he had obviously consumed before coming home. I would frequently hear Mom say, always in an exasperated tone, "He's likely stopped off at the Elks Club for a drink, or had several drinks with one of his many clients on his way home." (Later, I wondered how she knew this, but I was not about to inquire.) She was angry. Her tone was condescending when she said, "Cliff, get to the dinner table right THIS MINUTE. Dinner is getting cold!" We ate having minimal conversation. As soon as my dad started slurring his words while trying to pontificate, once again about some obscure topic, I, as a cocky teenager, pounced on his inappropriate behavior. I mocked him. I shamed him. I mistakenly thought it would make him behave better. Fat chance! It just made matters worse.

I did not know that my dad's jerk-like behavior at the dinner table was one of the signs of addiction. All I knew was dinner time was *beyond stressful.* I wanted to hurry through the meal, do the dishes, and retreat to my room...completely dismissing what had just happened.

While Dad was realizing his biggest dream, his mother, Alta, had married for the fourth time. I remember the only occasion when she came to our home for dinner. I was stunned once I opened the front door to greet her. With a cigarette dangling from her ruby red lips, she brashly said, "Well, look at you, every time I see you, your hair is a different color!" I looked at her feeling quietly disgusted, then wondered, "Who in the world is this person?" There were no niceties such as, "Hi, honey, how are you?" or maybe, "It's been a long time since I've seen you." Nope. Just the comment about my hair color, which was not any different than it had ever been. What an odd thing to say, especially since I never remembered meeting her before now. I heard a critical voice in my head say, *"Talk about hair color...her dyed black hair is way too dark. Look at her bright red lipstick, way too red placed well outside of her lip line."* Taking a breath, I slowly started smiling to myself. For in that moment I realized we were in for an interesting night. Despite my perverse excitement, I managed to regain my inner composure to become a dutiful daughter (for the moment), and quietly stepped aside for my dad to greet her.

As the evening progressed, never once did Alta show interest in anyone else. Once we sat down for dinner in our lovely dining room, she never stopped talking or smoking. She lit one cigarette off of another, the ashes falling on her dinner plate, into her food, eventually landing on the white damask tablecloth. Nothing stopped her from dominating the conversation. She talked on and on.

Laughably, for once, my dad could not get a word in edgewise. As his teenage daughter (who by that time could hardly get a word in edgewise unless I dominated the conversation the way he did), I reveled in watching his mother out-talk him. I was gleefully entertained by what I saw. However, Mom quietly seethed. She was disgusted by the scene as it unfolded. She had fixed a lovely dinner, as usual, except it went unnoticed by Alta. All that mattered to Alta was being the center of attention, having another cigarette and, of course, another drink.

I later discovered that two years prior to this visit, when Alta was 63, she and her husband had been arrested for public drunkenness. Though I was not aware of this at the time of her visit, I am guessing my parents might have been. Years later, I found the arrest record online. I felt sick as I stared at the document.

There on the arrest ledger was her name, her husband's name, the courthouse location, followed by the name of the judge who heard their case. The final column indicated the sentence: pay a $50 fine or spend ten days in jail. They chose jail. I was suddenly aware the family story about this was not a myth after all. I sat in shock for what seemed like hours. I calculated and realized she had been in her 60s. What in the world had she been doing with her life, I wondered? This was clearly addiction. Now, I ask Alta to reflect on this devastating event. *"I knew no other way to live. Alcohol seemed to erase everything I didn't like in my life. Jail took my life to a very low level. I wanted something different. I had little idea how to make it happen."* Before hearing her words, I wanted to disown Alta. I wanted to distance myself from how she lived. I wanted to pretend she had no connection to me. Now hearing her story, I also felt a sense of despair due to what she had endured. It was sad in every way.

Anyone looking at a picture taken of Dad and his mom the night she visited our home would never suspect the entangled history in their shared 45 years. They sat together on the sofa in our living room, Alta neatly dressed in a navy and white polka dotted blouse with navy skirt and jacket. (The camera's distance blurs her make-up and hair color.) Dad is dressed in his usual golf attire of casual shirt with slacks. He has his arm around his mother's shoulders; she has her hand gently resting on his leg. Both are smiling looking happy. Missing is any hint of early childhood neglect, drunken fights, along with a fragmented family life that left Dad and his brother estranged from their sisters. Absent is Alta's history of alcoholism or her arrest record. No hint of her serial marriages, the number of which was rarely discussed by family members. When the topic did come up, it was accompanied by much rolling of eyes mixed with laughter. On the contrary, I felt the deeper meaning not being expressed behind their superficial laughter. I clearly felt in Dad's eyes it was never a laughing matter.

The first and only visit to our home by Dad's mom around 1963.
She's pictured here with Dad after dinner.

In time, Mom became even more vigilant about Dad's drinking. Curious to find out why even on weekends with an early dinner hour, he still appeared drunk, she soon discovered he hid bottles of liquor everywhere. Whenever he left to run an errand, she scoured the house and garage. She usually found most of the bottles of alcohol hidden in the drawers of his work bench in the garage. In a fleeting moment of gaining control, she either emptied them, or added water to what liquor was already there. Not knowing what else to do, she faithfully adhered to the ritual of making sure Dad ate three good meals every day (dinner was always being served early). After dinner, she made sure he did not take any business calls as a way to protect him from making poor decisions for his customers. She also tried (futilely), to make sure he did not drive under the influence.

My dad prided himself on being articulate. He was an excellent conversationalist (as long as he was not drunk and you did not mind him dominating the conversation). On several occasions, Mom and I actually tape-recorded Dad's drunk conversations while at the dinner table. We thought this would be the perfect way to prove to him he was not very intelligible while under the influence (something he never believed possible no matter how many times we later told him). This experiment went sideways. Once we played the recording back to him the next day, he was furious. We had confronted a reality he did not want to see. Underneath his anger was surely shame (we saw what he did not want us to see), but his anger won out. Instantly, we became the enemy.

Mom's comments were usually restrained. She preferred action to abate the situation. When this strategy no longer worked, she lashed out at my dad. On these occasions, little was left unsaid. He reacted in kind for a moment. Once his fury lessened, it was as if nothing had happened. We all went our separate ways, me to my room, Mom to their bedroom, followed by my dad to the family room to watch TV. As I look back at the progression of Dad's addiction, it amazes me that never once was he physically abusive to either of us (as his father had been to him). Many nights he just sat down in front of the TV, and quietly passed out.

Typical for most children in alcoholic families, I assumed more responsibility. I dutifully calmed the emotional waters just as I had as a child. I made sure to help Mom prepare the meals. I always did the dishes (not happily), leaving the kitchen spotless. I became compulsive about cleaning. It was my way of controlling one of the few things I could control. I also became obsessed by keeping things in order. There was hardly a drawer or countertop in our home that was not perfectly arranged. I thought that would make Mom happy. It did not. She just griped about never being able to find anything.

In self-defense, I began to address Dad's alcoholic behavior more frequently. I did not let him dominate the conversation. I was pointed. And clear. When he was decidedly drunk, I left the room, refusing to engage. On those occasions, I usually went to bed not saying good night to either of my parents. That was my way of making my position clear. In the end, all I wanted was for Mom to feel supported, and for Dad to stop drinking. Underneath it all, the only thing that changed was my mounting sense of loneliness and isolation.

We were swimming in the waters of denial in characteristic naïveté. This well-developed, highly-organized, and sophisticated system kept us protected from the truth of seeing our deepest fears for many years. The reason it did was partly due to the fact that Dad's drinking did not always appear to be a problem. He had days when he was quite normal, always fun to be around. He was a highly functional alcoholic most of the time, running his very successful company, perfecting his golf game while seemingly enjoying life. The times when Dad appeared normal, we were seductively lulled into thinking he could control his drinking, or even go without.

We lacked a depth of understanding about addiction, leaving us blinded to the problem. We thought if we told him how much we enjoyed him when he did not drink, emphasizing how much fun we had on family outings when drinking was absent, he would change. A short truce always escalated into him "tying one on," as he used to say. It might happen at Christmas time, his birthday, my birthday, after a fabulous game of golf, or any other joyful time (yes, ironically, joyful times were the worst). When that happened, Mom and I were devastated. You name it, we felt it: anger, outrage, disappointment, powerlessness, embarrassment. By far the worst, however, was being *deceived.*

The more this happened, the more my emotional footing shifted, like being caught in a swirling undertow; I was constantly forced to re-balance, as best I could. I reacted by continuing to be outspoken. I turned to my friends and school as an outlet. Mom reacted by withdrawing. I wondered what it was like for her. Taking care of others was not new to Mom. Her caretaking had begun in her mid to late 20s with Penny. Similarly, when Mom saw that her nephew, Michael, (her younger sister's son) needed academic support in school, she made sure he got the tutoring he needed to succeed. She got his eyes tested, ensuring he had the prescription glasses he needed.

She was always there for them. While I was still in high school, she became a constant support to her mother, my Illinois grandmother, once she came to our home to live.

My dad adored my Grandmother Edith, for she was the mother he had never had. Fortunately, he was quite happy with the arrangement. What effect was this having on Mom, though? She already had my dad to worry about. Now she also had to attend to the additional responsibility for Grandma Edith's well-being.

With my mom constantly preoccupied, I remember having no one in my family to whom I could consistently turn. I was very grateful to feel physically safe, yet I rarely felt emotionally secure. Coupled with loneliness and isolation, I see in retrospect how a growing sense of restlessness and negativity developed. I was critical about everything and everyone, especially at home. Bottom line: I wanted my world to be different.

Little did I realize while the waters I swam in were helping me gain greater insight into others' needs and wants, they prevented me from having any self-perception. At any given moment, I did not know what I needed, wanted, or even felt. Most of the time, I was highly dependable. When I could no longer bear this burden, I lashed out at one or both of my parents, often over something trivial. I did not mince words about what I did not like. Once said, I did not wait for a response. I just marched down the hallway to retreat in my bedroom, slamming the door behind me. If you had asked me what I felt at the time, I would have had no idea.

Later, Mom would come to my room to offer support. For the moment I felt heard, gaining some insight to what I felt. Rarely, if ever, did Dad attempt to reconcile with me. I knew he was annoyed by my contemptuous behavior toward him. A big part of me did not care. One morning while sitting at the breakfast table, I was sullen, disgusted by his drunkenness from the night before. He tried to carry on a superficial conversation with me, but I did not budge from my position. As I sat reviewing last night's horror with him, it was obvious he did not know what I was talking about. His lack of awareness ignited my persistence but to no avail. His stern look turned to steel when he said: "That's enough. I'll talk to you when you're worth talking to. Come back when you're ready to be part of this family. Right now, I have no idea who you are." On the one hand, I was glad I had provoked him. On the other hand, however, I felt the sharp sting of his words. Even though I wanted to lash out at him, putting him in his place once and for all, I was silenced, for the shame shook any semblance I had of feeling loved and valued by him.

Chapter 6

Lifelines

As high school came to a close, I was eager to create my own life, on my own terms. (Yes, just like my dad had done.) I focused on my future, burying any feelings of rejection I felt by my dad. College was my ticket. I was accepted at Oregon State University in the fall of 1964. Knowing it would be hard to meet new people as a "townie" (one who went to high school and college in the same town), and not living on campus for most of first year, my close high school friend, Carolyn, and I decided to go through the sorority rush system before classes began as a way to be more connected to campus life. The experience was a success. We both gained new friendships during the week of rush plus we ended up pledging sororities not far from one another.

I loved being in college, especially once I could live in my sorority. I rarely went home except for holidays or summer break. Despite my early and deep bond with my dad, now 18 years later, he was a total stranger, a man I hardly knew. Instead of dwelling on this, I focused on the opportunities before me. I began to find various forms of support, the first being through new friendships. Each friendship anchored me, bringing a welcome sense of belonging. The more friends I gained the easier it was for my family's circumstances to fade into the background.

Having gained greater emotional maturity and confidence during college helped me see more of what was actually happening between my parents once I was home. There was definitely an "elephant in the room." We danced around it, unable to name it. Mom's emotional well-being clearly showed signs of wear. In addition to the stress created by Dad's chronic drinking, she was fraught with guilt from having to move her beloved mother to a local care facility. Grandma Edith had developed dementia and her care needs had become too great. Mom chose the better of the two care facilities in town, but that did not ease her guilt. It just ate away at her. My dad maintained his preoccupations found in focusing on the success of his business and playing golf. By the time I finished college and moved out on my own to begin a teaching position in town, we had firmly established three separate realities that rarely touched one another. It took Grandma Edith's life-threatening crisis a few months later to momentarily halt that.

The call came from the nursing home one day, saying Grandma had just broken her hip. (She had gotten her foot caught in the tall metal railing at the end of her bed; her twisting had fractured her pelvis.) The protocol at the time was surgery, regardless of age, and my parents complied with the doctor's decision. Surgery was immediately scheduled. It was a late summer morning when I walked into the hospital waiting room to be with Mom during Grandma's surgery. She was visibly distraught, barely looking at me once I sat down. "Where's Dad?" I asked. With a tone seething of resentment, she quietly replied, "In spite of Grandma's surgery, he chose to keep his usual day of playing golf. After all, he couldn't disappoint his foursome." I was livid. He was such an asshole. Time away from them had given me an even greater perspective. I had noticed how self-centered he was, consumed by his own life, at the forefront of which was golf. At this moment, I had no interest in what mattered to him. All that mattered to me was what was best for Mom. I thought about the situation for a few minutes, then with fury fuelling a quiet resolve, I told Mom I was going to the restroom. Instead, I went to a public phone in the hospital lobby. I called the country club where he was playing golf. "There's been an emergency in my family," I calmly said. "I need to speak to Cliff Culley as soon as possible. I'll hold while someone locates him." Ten minutes later he came to the phone. When he said hello, his voice reflected annoyance, but I did not care. I immediately launched into my irritation: "Why aren't you at the hospital at this critical time?" He lamely replied: "Honey, there isn't anything I can do there." Not missing a beat, I spit out my words: "*Grandma is 80* years old and having a very serious surgery. Did it occur to you she might not make it?" Leaving no time for his reply, I pressed on, saying, "Even if she does pull through, Mom needs your support, no matter what!" His words sputtered a bit, as he tried to find a way to defend his actions. I ignored his attempt, instead I blurted out in a steely tone, "Get here now!"

When he walked into the hospital waiting room, Mom was shocked. For a fleeting moment, she abandoned all restraint, let out a gasp of surprise, and jumped into his arms, something I had not witnessed for quite some time. I could see how deeply touched she was to have him by her side. I hoped Dad could see that as well. Secretly, I doubted it. (He truly had become an assaholic, a term I had recently created for him. Now he was a man I truly did not want to know.) Even if he did not get the importance of supporting Mom, at least he was there. That was all that mattered to me. For that brief moment, our three realities had fleetingly intersected.

Most of the time, however, we lived parallel lives. When I did visit, the knot in my stomach resumed its role of signaling the emotional climate of the moment. When it tightened, I knew I needed to protect myself. These cumulative observations revealed the ongoing emotional wreckage that was becoming reality for my parents' marriage. I often found myself frantic, searching my mind for the right thing to do. I occasionally tried to lighten things up, or attempted to be a good listener for Mom, while trying to set clear boundaries for myself, yet sometimes it was simply easier to pretend not to see all that was going on. Most of the time, my thoughts tended towards resignation, feeling there was little I could do. Rarely did I leave not feeling utterly helpless. It was the water I swam in. It deeply illustrated the very up-close and personal nature of addiction.

Our worst fear was realized when early one morning I came to the house to go for a walk with Mom. As we started down the driveway she suddenly stopped, letting out a gasp. I turned to see what had caught her attention. In that moment, we found ourselves staring at the neighbor's car parked next to the sidewalk, a long gash of contrasting orange paint gaping at us along its side. What was even more alarming was that it just so happened to be an exact match to

Dad's car. Could it be my dad had been involved in this unthinkable action? We aborted our walk to examine his car, confirming our suspicions: he had indeed sideswiped the neighbor's car on his way home from work the night before. And since he had not mentioned it to Mom when he arrived home, alcohol had clearly made him completely oblivious to what he had done. His driving while drunk had always been our worst nightmare. Now, it could not be denied.

Mom had despair written all over her face. She had tolerated his bad behavior for years. There had been occasional outbursts, but she had mostly bottled it up inside. Today was different. She was fed up, which galvanized her despair into action. We marched into the house to find Dad at the breakfast table. "There's something you need to see...now," she said with authority. Once outside, she showed him his car then the neighbor's car. "You need to take care of this immediately. And I mean it, Cliff!" There it was, plain as day. Wordless, Mom went back into the house. My dad stood there, looking contrite. Absent of argument or fanfare, he later took care of the damage done. But in typical fashion, the incident was never spoken of again.

Their life went on, quiet desperation mounting. Despite this, my life, by appearances, was productive. After two years of teaching high school, I married my college boyfriend in 1970. With the Vietnam War in full force, and a compulsory draft in place, my new husband saw no other choice at the time than to become an officer in the military. As a result, we spent five years traveling from one state to the next for flight training followed by his eventual tour of Vietnam. The late 1960s and early 1970s were a tumultuous time in our country, with war, protests, and assassinations resulting in major social upheaval. In a way, it seemed to parallel the path of my family.

My few visits home during that time left me raw. I either felt sad or mad. Even though my parents were busy with travel and their social circle, the depths of their emotional sands were constantly shifting as Dad's addiction worsened. I learned to *never* trust the outward appearance of my family through careful attention to the more subtle details. Even though my visits were brief, I noticed words that did not match behavior. At the breakfast table, I took stock of the yellow film over Dad's eyes, the redness that veined through their whites. I knew he was hung over. "How are you today?" I would ask. "Oh, I'm fine, honey. Going to work soon. It's going to be a busy day." Translation: He feels awful but believes he is in control. He is convinced today will not be a repeat of yesterday. Work will focus him. Overhearing this conversation, Mom would ask when he would be home for dinner, her body stiff, her tone sharp. Translation: You better not drink while at work or stop off anywhere on the way home. I do not want to see you drunk one more time. Keep it together, for once. Every time I witnessed this type of exchange, I felt the deeper truth rumbling beneath me like a seismic wave, threatening at any moment to fracture the tenuous crust of denial we stood upon.

Even though I was always relieved to leave their home, the constant ache of utter powerlessness remained a constant. I was keenly aware my family was unraveling at an increasingly greater rate. I had no idea how to break the cycle of this vicious predicament.

When the Vietnam War finally ended, we settled in Virginia while my husband completed the last two years of his military commitment. I set my sights on taking the classes needed to renew my teaching credential, which had lapsed due to our constant relocations. Instead, to my surprise, a series of events unfolded leading me to pursue a master's degree in counseling.

For the first time, now in graduate school, I experienced what a positive difference it made to love what I was learning from those who loved what they taught. I was personally mentored from the moment I began my first class until I graduated. I loved every class I took, especially classes on addiction. Now, my eyes were wide open to what was happening in my family. It finally had a name: *alcoholism.* I became passionate about the subject, reading everything available. Gaining knowledge about what my family was embroiled in gave me the long-awaited clarity I sought. Even though it was not what I wanted to see, the truth empowered me.

Once my husband left the military, we moved back to Oregon, living near my parents in Corvallis. In time, I got my dream job working as a counselor at a local community college. What joy it was to love what I was doing, to work with colleagues who valued emotional truth and healing. I found myself right where I needed to be to thrive.

Feeling empowered by what I continued to learn about addiction, I was eager to attend an Al-Anon meeting. I also wanted Mom to accompany me. Despite her resistance, I persisted. I knew she was even more resigned to Dad's addiction than ever. I wanted that to change. My tenacity finally paid off when she agreed to join me at a local meeting.

At our first meeting, I immediately realized I had found a home of kindred spirits. We all had one thing in common: we loved an alcoholic. I found the information empowering. My heart was touched by the stories shared by many of the members. We were united by this horrible disease. I was no longer *alone*. Sadly, Mom's experience was distinctly different. She was resolute that one did not share their "dirty laundry" in public, let alone with strangers at an Al-Anon meeting (regardless of the strict guidelines around confidentiality in all meetings). She was visibly anxious when hearing many of the "secrets" only known to us behind closed doors, now being mirrored by others and disclosed by them in such a public way. The more others shared, the more restless she became.

In contrast, I felt set free. Finally, the truth was being spoken. Here was courage. Here was support. Sadly, it would never offer that to Mom. While walking out to the car after the meeting I noticed she struggled to catch her breath, seeming to be on the verge of a panic attack. Once in the car she became more settled. I gathered my thoughts as we both sat in silence for a few minutes then said with a newfound enthusiasm: "I loved hearing others' stories. I felt so connected. What was your experience?" Her tone was surprisingly resigned, and unspeakably sad when she uttered, "I never want to go back to that meeting or any other meeting ever again." I was shocked. I wanted her to share my experience, to feel supported, and connected. Regrettably she did not. She invoked a code of silence, so common in alcoholic families. Even though I tried to learn more about her experience later that night, and in the weeks to follow, she rarely said another word. When I occasionally asked, she would look at me with a stern resolve and leave the room in silence.

The only exception came a month later. After I stopped by their house to drop off some things, we sat down to visit for a few minutes. Suddenly, out of nowhere, she blurted out: "You're a counselor now. You're the only one who can get your father to stop drinking!" I sat there, speechless. We had not been talking about my dad or his drinking. It was obvious she could not contain her growing desperation from her day to day reality. After a few deep breaths to find the right words, I slowly answered, relying on all I had read about the disease. "It's not all up to me, Mom. I know you think it is. It is not. This is a family disease." Feeling more confident, I emphasized, "We need to be equally informed and equally determined to intervene with Dad's drinking." I was not sure where my strength was coming from but somehow I felt clear and determined. I was not going to be made to feel responsible for fixing him. I had carried sufficient responsibility long enough. Finally, I ended by saying, "We need to see where we are enabling him. We need to correct this, no longer tolerating another day of his drinking. It will be the only way." Despite feeling confident I was shaking inside. This topic was so loaded for me. It took a few minutes before Mom replied. Contempt then filled her voice as she spit out her final words on the subject: "This has nothing to do with me!"

My heart sank, the shock numbing me. Mom had made her position clear. Once again, I was chillingly alone watching my family erode away. Was it really all up to me? I was now an army of one fighting for my family. After returning home and reflecting, I realized I was not only fighting for my family, I was also fighting for *my life.* I could not let this disease take hold of me as it had my parents. I had to claim my own life. I had to claim my right to emancipate myself from this bondage in order to begin my own healing process.

Al-Anon became my constant support. Sometimes, I would sit in the back of the room, not saying a word, just listening. It was there I appreciated the simple presence of everyone in attendance. I had such admiration for their courage and strength. Initially, I was saddened by their pain in loving an alcoholic. Only over time could I slowly begin to recognize, then finally feel, compassion for my own emotional pain, the likes of which I had endured for too many years.

With the establishment of these vital lifelines, I was now ready to move out of the darkness that alcoholism had created in my life. I had support from Al-Anon, my colleagues, the knowledge gained from my academic training and the many books I had read, all by my side. In time, I began to see the healing power secretly held within the adversity of this disease.

Unknown to me, the laying of this foundation was well-timed, as my challenge lay directly ahead: alcoholism was about to become one of my greatest teachers.

Chapter 7

Failed Attempts

A l-Anon gave me a clear set of guidelines from which to live. I got a firm grip on what alcoholism was, and how it affected me as well as my parents. Knowing alcoholism was a family disease, I was committed to my own recovery, now recognizing I was a product of an alcoholic father. I resonated with descriptions written about adult children from alcoholic families. I was an over-achiever on the outside next to being a lonely, depressed person on the inside. As Claudia Black wrote in her book, *It Will Never Happen to Me*, the hallmarks of being an adult from an alcoholic family (ACA/ACOA) are: don't trust, don't feel, and don't talk. I could relate to each. The more I learned, the more empowered I became. It was not easy, though. All it took for me to backslide was seeing my dad. The effects of his drinking were taking an ever-increasing toll, witnessed by his obvious ongoing physical and cognitive deterioration. He now had high blood pressure mixed with periodontal disease, among other things. It was difficult for him to handle high-level cognitive tasks. Yet even with these deteriorations, it was a wonder there was not more.

It was not much easier to see Mom, either. Not a problem drinker herself, by any means, but living with one was a jail sentence. I could see the effects of constant worry and aggravation now permanently etched on her face. I had watched my once independent-minded Mom slowly learn to be helpless (so common for family members) by living in the constant traumatic environment of addiction. There were moments when I felt her on the edge of emotional collapse. She had a hard time taking action or moving forward; she seemed chronically stuck. Desperately wanting to help her, I shared what I was learning. Family members were affected in very distinct ways, a fact that had been ignored for many years. I wanted her to realize this, for her to know she was not alone. She listened in silence. I rarely knew if I helped. I just knew I felt compelled to keep trying; hoping one day something positive might take hold.

The sadness of watching my parents being slowly encircled by the grip of addiction was a devastating constant. I saw the awfulness of it, the futility, and the waste. Watching their lives going nowhere good was like a prolonged, agonizing death. But somehow, deep down, I knew I had a choice: I could join them or I could let this disease teach me what I needed to learn in order to survive. I constantly leaned on the well-known Serenity Prayer for support. No matter where I was or what I was doing, its message always centered me. I could be innocently driving home from work when a replay of a recent conversation with Mom would unexpectedly interrupt my thoughts. Listening to her vent her powerlessness always triggered my own sense of powerlessness, free to arise only after I had removed myself from the situation. I would be flooded by emotion, causing me to find a private place to pull off to and park. At first, no words would come, just primitive sounds, followed by tears of helplessness. Once the emotion finally dissipated, I would open my purse and shuffle through many of my "lifeline cards," as I called them. On each card I had carefully written a word ("Breathe") or a statement ("Let Go and Let God") that would be my touchstone. Frequently, my touchstone was this part of the "Serenity Prayer":

God grant me the serenity to accept the things I cannot change, courage to change the things I can, and the wisdom to know the difference.

I would repeat it over and over until I felt soothed, once again finding my anchor.

Another inescapable reality of addiction was the tendency to go to the worst case scenario. What if this never ends? Or worse, what if my dad dies of this? These fears could suck the life right out of me, sending me back into desperation. It could surround and cripple me in a heartbeat, consuming my every waking moment, if I let it. Repeatedly, I would need to remember...go back to the Serenity Prayer.

As my healing progressed, I began to perceive from a new perspective that my dad had been an early- to mid-stage alcoholic for many years, able to function remarkably well in most aspects of his life. However, as I observed him in his late 50s to early 60s, it was easy to see he had begun to falter. Aside from what was happening within our family, friction developed between Dad and his long-time business partner. His partner wanted to invest in other unrelated start-up businesses. My dad wanted to keep their highly successful, unique, full-service agrichemical company growing.

Gone was my dad's ability to analyze this situation as a means of resolving the differences harmoniously, a once finely-honed skill set. Now that he was in the beginning stage of advanced alcoholism, he ruminated, agonizing over the situation for months. Even though my mercurial love/hate relationship persisted, I seamlessly went from being his emotionally estranged daughter to his friend and parent (one of my many ways of being co-dependent), as I remember the many nights we talked about this dilemma. I could see his angst; his desperation was palpable, for his dearly beloved company was in peril. But so was his ability to reason effectively. In the end, he finally recognized what had long been obvious to others, sadly ending the partnership. Later, when a Spokane corporation offered to buy his business, keeping him on as general manager, he saw it as a guarantee to infuse the company with additional money while remaining in the role he excelled at best. Little did he know his vision was quite shortsighted.

Within a year of new ownership, executives from the company began their cruel, but effective, tactics to remove Dad as manager. I was mortified to witness him being clueless about their intentions. Seeing this glaring obliviousness, I used the opportunity to chip away at his denial: "Dad, alcohol has clearly taken over your life. In the past, you would have handled this difficult situation with aplomb. Now, you can't think clearly. Not like you used to. This is alcoholism. The progression of this disease will surely end your life." To openly admit (let alone imagine) he might die of this disease was brutally agonizing for me. But I had steeled myself to the possibility months before. "Al-Anon is a part of my life now," I said. "AA could be a part of yours." I finished by saying, "You know, in the end, it's all up to you." Even though my words were clear, my body was a quivering mess. Inside, I was reeling from the intensity of it all. I was desperately hoping my words could get through to him.

He quietly nodded in agreement. For the next few days he did not drink. Then as if he had discovered a newfound strategy, he reverted back to his old set of rules around drinking, limiting himself to two drinks a day. Not realizing he could not outwit the disease through *moderation*, his alcoholic drinking was rapidly back in full swing.

Eventually, Dad woke up to the fact that he was being pressured to leave, and finally did so, after 20 years of co-owning and managing his company. He received a fair severance package, leaving the company in the hands of his valued assistant, who took his place as manager. Anxious to keep working, Dad did not waste any time processing what had happened. Even though I thought he needed to be more deliberate about considering his next step, he rushed into forming an immediate plan.

He started his own consulting business within weeks, continuing to work with many of the farm families he had served in the past (some of which had now grown into large corporations). Consulting was a daunting challenge he could not fully grasp, but Mom did. The increased liability of his being a private consultant while impaired by limited cognitive functioning posed a high level of risk. Mom was frantic. For years, she had fielded evening business calls, but now evening was the only window for calls with new and current clients, since most farmers spent their daylight hours in the field. By evening, Dad was not remotely capable of functioning. If he had not passed out while eating dinner, he was certain to afterwards.

Farmers relied on him to provide a full range of services, beginning with soil analysis and assessment. He suggested the best crops based on this information followed by recommending fertilizers and pesticides to optimize production. One mistake could cost thousands of dollars. The sad reality was he was in no shape to give solid advice to anyone at any time of day.

Soon an offer came which my parents could not refuse: the chance to move back to an active retirement community in sunny Southern California, where Mom's dearest friend, my now-widowed godmother, Dottie, lived. Mom jumped at the chance, although it was not easy for my dad, who would have to let go of his fledgling consulting business. Just as they were preparing to move, I got a job offer that I could not refuse. Within a few months, my parents moved to California, and my husband and I relocated to central Oregon. With the current of change flowed hope for better times, making it easy to forget the problems at hand.

Once my parents settled, Dad and the current manager of his previous company created an opportunity for him to work as a consultant in the southern California region (where his career had first begun). The only remaining problem: his ongoing drinking. My weekly phone conversations with Mom always ended with the same desperate plea: "Please help your father! He's gotten so bad. You have no idea how bad it is here." Sometimes, her pleas could hook me. I could feel guilty for not doing enough. I could feel like a failure. When I unhooked from the guilt, I could remind myself, once again, that this was not about me, it was about him. I gave her information about AA. I impressed upon her the importance of investigating various treatment facilities. If and when the time came, she would need to act swiftly and decisively. My words fell on deaf ears; she was frozen in fear, like a deer in the headlights. At those times, I wanted to shake her (from 1000 miles away). I wanted her to wake up, take charge of this untenable situation. She just could not. My deeply ingrained sense of responsibility left me feeling the weight of it all.

My body belied the knowing I had in my mind that it was not all up to me: my stomach constantly ached from the ongoing turmoil; my neck and shoulders held a tight grip from carrying the weight of this nightmare. In an instant, I could be seized by a sickening disgust of the whole situation. Even deeper was my ever-present sense of powerlessness. It could enrage me, or it could reduce me to tears. I was living my life between a rock and a hard place. And I **hated** it.

The best way for me to express my accumulated anger and frustration was to go for a run. In these times, I hurriedly pulled on my running shoes, put a leash on my faithful dog, Sadie, and ran until all pent-up emotion was spent. As the sweat dripped down my face, for a long moment it felt glorious to be free of what haunted me.

When I caught my breath, I would turn to this lifeline card, these words from Al-Anon, to keep me afloat: *I didn't cause this, I can't control it, and I can't cure it.*

Yet I remained steadfast in my resolve to support my dad's effort to become sober. I gave him the number for AA chapters in his new community. I sent him literature to read. But I knew I could not advise any further. The sad agonizing truth was he would have to hit bottom. My work was to recognize then accept responsibility for my own anxiety.

Our move to central Oregon was positive, at first. I continued to love my work as a community college counselor. Now living in the heart of Oregon's recreational center brought new opportunities to hike, bike and ski, all an added bonus for both me and my husband. Hidden in the shadows, though, were unresolved issues from the past that caught up with us. Like many who served in combat during the Vietnam War, he experienced symptoms of PTSD and these were left untreated. That, along with the surfacing of my unmet emotional needs fostered by the emotional chaos that my family's alcoholism bred, brought us to counseling as a way to sort through the confusion. Sadly, in the end, I left my husband. Despite the separation, I was committed to my personal work with my counselor to further unpack the mental compartment containing the many things I could not face when I was younger. Now in my early 30s, my deeper family trauma was about to be addressed.

A valuable outcome from counseling was learning about the coping strategy of compartmentalizing as a way to live with my dad's addiction. Although I was completely unaware of choosing this strategy years before, I saw where I had used it to neatly package all the feelings from positive events into one box in my mind while sealing away all those negative and messy things I did not know what to do with into another. Two different boxes: one locked, one not locked. Compartmentalizing created a type of amnesia about feelings that were confusing, difficult and painful, allowing me to have some semblance of emotional balance. The contents of the two boxes were never meant to meet. This coping strategy had been quite effective at limiting my memory during those years, probably functioning as protection from what I had not been able to manage. But it had also limited my perspective. In fact, it had worked so well that I could not remember much about my dad's drinking during adolescence. Surely it was present (because alcoholism does not happen overnight), but why the gap in my memory? The answer came in the form of a wonderful high school friend years later. Sandy had been my first friend when I transferred to Corvallis High School as a sophomore. Singing together in Girls' Glee everyday cemented our relationship, as we were routinely scolded for giggling in the back row while the conductor was talking. Our teacher was rarely happy with our behavior, but we were often excused because of our much-needed musical ability. We had easily remained lifetime friends from that moment on. We had a chance meeting years later when both of us were going through divorces and she a career change. She was attending a weekend workshop near where I lived so we met for dinner. I told her about my focus in therapy as it related to my dad's drinking sharing that I had few, if any memories, of his drinking while in high school. She was surprised by this, swiftly offering her perspective. "Do you remember when you asked me to spend the night at your house only later for you to call me back to tell me not to come because your dad was drunk?" Her question left me visibly shaken for I had absolutely no memory of this. Then she added, "You talked about his drinking a lot while we were in high school, Pam. And I saw it for myself, as well, when I would be at your house. I always felt bad for you. I knew how much you loved your dad, and I did, too, but he had a problem." Sandy's perspective served as my key to unlocking my past. Because of her I was able to let myself remember more of the many crises that had occurred during those years that I had not been able to let myself see until now. She was my cherished and much-needed witness during those challenging years.

I grew stronger as I continued therapy. Even though I swam in the waters of addiction, I learned to set better boundaries. I became better at the ongoing process of not absorbing or taking responsibility for Mom's feelings. I learned how to establish and maintain a more solid, emotional footing. All of my newly acquired skills would soon be put to an even greater challenge which came once my parents asked me to spend the upcoming Christmas holiday with them. Immediately, I recognized it for the red flag it was: a situation fraught with trouble. For many years, holidays, including Christmas, had been just an excuse for Dad to drink to excess. It never ended well. I definitely was not interested in returning to that scene. Even though I wanted to see them, I did not want to be stuck 1000 miles away from home, if or when Dad's drinking was out of control. Thinking it through, and getting ideas from my counselor, I broached this dilemma with my parents on the phone. Being clear about how much I wanted to see them, I was also equally clear about the effect Dad's drinking had on me. "I won't tolerate another holiday ruined by your drinking, Dad. It breaks my heart every time this happens. If it happens while I'm there, I will shorten my visit and leave immediately. And I mean it!" Both said they understood, but I was not sure they really believed it. As I made plans to visit, I was hoping for the best while knowing I had to be strong enough to follow through with my early departure plan, if the worst should occur.

At the beginning of my visit, Dad abstained from drinking. In its absence, we became more open and relaxed as a family. It was wonderful. We had such fun, for it was a return to our earlier years. It also created an opportunity for me and Dad to have some meaningful time together. In the early years, before alcohol became central, we could talk about anything, whether we were working on a project together or discussing current events in the car.

Over time my heart had become numbed by countless disappointments from the many years of betrayal plus abandonment that only alcoholism can foster. I was deeply distrustful that the joy of our earlier years could *ever* return. Our daily walks began to create an opening for us. Slowly, our connection returned. At the right moment, once again, I talked about alcohol's devastation on all of us. He listened. nodding his head in full agreement. I turned to him, holding his hands in mine, saying: "Dad, I love you! I so want what's best for you. I want you to want that, too. Drinking has made you depressed and impossible to live with. I've felt I lost you years ago. Is it too much to ask you to return?" In that moment, our hearts, having been closed to one another for so many years, began to open. Our deep abiding love timidly peeked out from the shadows. Despite the severe hardship imposed by addiction, we felt a tenderness return, the joy of this gift reflected by our mutual tears.

It was a precious, but fleeting moment, however. I overlooked a key fact: alcoholics suffer from an illness they cannot control. Even though I had more awareness about this disease than Mom, I fell into the trap of magical thinking, suggesting that somehow my dad was different (stronger, smarter, more aware) from every other alcoholic. Sadly, yet predictably, his abstinence did not last. It simply could not. The next day he started drinking again, only this time it was worse than ever. He only had one drink before he passed out. My utter devastation, now having reached an unimaginable low, left me completely spent. My heart was shattered. The fleeting moment of our deep father-daughter bond was shredded, leaving nothing but a sickening, bitter aftertaste.

I wanted to deny what had happened, dismiss it, rationalize it, pretend it would not happen again, but I could not. I had made a promise to myself. That night, I went to my bedroom, closed the door to quietly call the airline, requesting a flight change. Once in place, with a stern resolve nesting in my aching heart, I told my parents I was leaving in the morning. The scene was quietly gruesome. Momentarily, Mom dropped her stoic nature, tearfully pleading with me not to go. Dad said nothing, but his eyes revealed his understanding and his shame. After I packed my things, I sat on the bed in a stupor reeling from everything that had just transpired. Swiftly, reality hit. I wept until there were no more tears to shed. My worst-case scenario had happened. The unfamiliarity of doing the right thing felt awful. I was full of guilt, then anger. For a fleeting, twisted moment, my ego weighed in to insist I had failed. I soon overruled what I heard, strengthening my resolve. No longer was I going to abandon myself, as I had in the past, in favor of my parents' needs. In spite of my family's situation, I was doing what I needed to support myself. I was clear and unwavering: me, first.

Now as I write this, I hear Mom saying she has something to share with me from spirit. I am grateful for whatever she wants to add since the effect of alcoholism was rarely a topic she wanted to discuss when she was here. *"I was devastated by your leaving. I admired your courage to do so. I longed to have the same resolve, but was overwhelmed by it all. Don't for a moment ever think I didn't value your strength, your stamina to see this through."* I take a deep breath hearing these words for the very first time. As they sink in I feel a weight being lifted from my heart, the one attached to a past belief that she could still be angry with me for my actions, even hurt that I chose my well-being over hers.

The next day, I numbly went through the motions of going to the airport and boarding the plane. I was on automatic pilot, void of any feelings. Once on the plane, the floodgates opened; I cried all the way home. I could not seem to stop. I had just witnessed my parents at an all-time low; both desperately unhinged. I could not get the image out of my mind. It shook me to my core to see these dear people, my parents, completely taken over by the effects of addiction.

Once home, I returned to my counselor who, once again, offered a crucial lifeline of support. I learned I was at a critical juncture in my healing. It was now time to take it to the next level. I slowly let my emotions lead the way. Some weeks I screamed, some weeks I wailed. The most important lesson at the time was realizing the key to healing was in understanding, then having compassion for, the pain I had carried. With these as my foundation, I could release it. Week after week, I went to counseling, digging deeper each time. As I looked back, I realized that what I had witnessed while at my parents' home had been deeply traumatizing. In the past, I would not have been prepared to see this. Now I was. However, leaving prematurely, for the reason I did, was the hardest thing I had EVER done.

Chapter 8

The Miracle of Recovery

The trauma of the Christmas ordeal engulfed me in agitation, expressing as irritation across my life. I was not happy with myself, at work, or with friends. Upon closer examination, the core source of my agitation was really about Dad's drinking; every time I replayed the worst parts of the Christmas visit, it burned like fire in the pit of my stomach, making me jump out of my skin. My dad's addiction was at its peak, with a central theme in my own life of rarely feeling seen or heard by him for long. Our moment of renewed connection was now long gone. I seethed a slow-burning anger at feeling invisible. How dare he not hear me! Does he not know how he is impacting me and Mom? He's such an assaholic! In one more attempt to connect, I wrote a letter a few weeks later (which I later found in his papers after his death). Once again, I told him how very difficult it was to see him struggling with the perils of addiction. "There isn't any way you can stop drinking by yourself, Dad. There isn't any way around it. No amount of rationalizing, intellectualizing or conning yourself will diminish the truth. It hurts me to see you when you're drinking. I don't want to know you or be around you." I pleaded by saying, "Please, do what you know you need to do." I finished by saying "You have my love always." As I read over the letter, I was surprised to see myself say that he had my love. I wondered how that had been even remotely possible given the circumstances. I sat with that question for days. The addiction had broken my heart for countless years. My family had been held hostage for decades. The answer came as I re-read a paragraph from one of my many books on the subject. It made a critical distinction between the disease and the person. Knowing this, I realized I still loved *him*... but not his *alcoholic behavior*. Yes, our early bond of love had emerged as unbreakable, despite all that had happened. However, could the situation become even more intolerable to the point I would not care to separate him from the addiction? I sat in dread of this possibility.

I was becoming well acquainted with my varied reactions to his addiction. The more I learned, the more aware I became, allowing better ways of coping to develop. But I could still be triggered. If it was not agitation, it was anger, which could take over, ruling my inner world. Sometimes, my anger boiled over. I was quick to judge others, especially men who displayed similar behavior to my dad's. Any arrogance, attitude of superiority over women, charm, or deception in their communication were the flags of a matador to my bull. I seized the moment to verbally charge. I was adept at poking holes in their well-articulated statements. I learned to be bigger and better than them. At the time, I thought this defense strategy would protect me from further personal injury. I reasoned it was certainly better than not doing anything. In the end, it only served to slowly seal off another layer of my heart.

Counseling deepened my awareness of this. Nevertheless, I did not *fully realize* how much of my thinking was about Dad's drinking as well as Mom's well-being. It had been second nature for so long I did not comprehend it was what I woke up to most mornings and went to sleep with most nights. My obsession to fix an irreparable situation began to find an outlet at work plus in some relationships. I over-functioned, eventually turning perfection into my drug of choice. The more effective I was, the better I felt. The more I accomplished and did for others, the happier I became; it momentarily relieved me of my chronic low-grade depression created by the many years of powerlessness I had experienced.

I became adept at controlling everything. I also became driven. I looked at many things through the lens of needing to be managed, whether they were situations, people, or even fun. If I could solve everything in front of me, I was elated. I felt adept mastering all I could. I was rewarded for this, too. But what would happen when I could not succeed? When I could not solve every problem (like Dad's chronic drinking), which was likely at some point? Tying all of my happiness to my accomplishments was fraught with danger. In the moment, it felt good—really good—for it provided a much-needed reprieve from the underlying, chronic disrepair in my family.

The negative impact of alcoholism endured, but also brought forth important lessons. It forced me to focus on my own recovery as well as self-care. I never doubted my decision to take care of me; it seemed built-in somehow. Learning about the concept of *healthy detachment* was key to releasing myself from bondage. When I first heard this term in an Al-Anon meeting, I was perplexed. How could I detach from someone I love? I soon learned that it is not detaching from those we care about, but from the *agony of the involvement* which usually takes the form of worry and obsession about *their* problems. Ideally, it is releasing or detaching from a person or problem *in love* so that they can be fully responsible for themselves, experiencing the natural consequences of their actions. This teaching resonated. I knew the concept was fundamental, for it provided me with additional support to better float in the waters of addiction; it was the air that filled my imaginary water-wings.

Learning I was responsible *only for myself* was another key concept. As basic as it might sound, it was a very different belief from what I had been raised with. I always thought I was responsible for my parents' well-being no matter how illogical it seemed. Understanding I was the only one I could be responsible for brought a much-needed sense of *relief*. As I applied this new concept, my life began to change. At times, I could let myself off the hook. I could enjoy the moment in spite of things around me not being perfect. I could let go of being serious, *allowing some spontaneity*. In time, I slowly began to relinquish both some regrets from the past and some fears about the future. Believe me, never did I do this alone. I always had the support I needed from friends, colleagues and those at Al-Anon meetings. Even with this, alongside ongoing professional support, it was a very uneven process. Three steps forward, two back, a process so common in recovery.

The phone call came just as I finished dinner one night. Once I answered, I immediately heard the strain in Mom's voice. "Oh, I so hope she's OK," I found myself thinking, already on the alert.

At first, her voice being so shaky, I could not follow what she was trying to say. Barely catching her breath, she practically whispered in the phone saying, "Your father...he... is... in... a... rehabilitation center. He went today." My mind raced. I wondered if I had heard her correctly. "He's where? In a rehab center?" Hesitating for a moment, she finally uttered, "Yes," still sounding very anxious. Why was she anxious about such a positive thing? Why was she not sounding relieved? After pausing to allow her to finish saying what little she strained to say while giving me time for it to sink in, I finally offered my perspective. "You know, Mom, this is exactly where he needs to be, right?" Haltingly, she said, "Well, yes, I guess." Pressing the point, "He's in good hands now, Mom. This is what we've always hoped for, isn't it?" "Yes," she finally said, "but I don't know what's going to happen next." I was stunned to learn Mom was frightened about what might happen next, when all I felt was RELIEF. Our differences were glaringly exposed once again. Even though I had more questions, such as what were the circumstances that led to this, Mom was done. I could hear it in her voice; my body tingled with her nervous energy. I reflected on a previous conversation several years before when she told me she never wanted to speak about Dad's addiction again. Now, she was forced to. For years, she had been accustomed to stuffing everything she did not want to think about into her own personal Pandora's Box. The lock was always secure. Now, it was not. On some level, I think she was terrified of losing control. It was a terror I knew too well, having experienced what was in my own Pandora's Box once I unlocked it. I had had many messy moments in my therapist's office where I could hardly believe what was coming out of my mouth. The depth of my disappointment next to my inability to control what was happening in my family was central. Again and again, I felt I could not fix anything thing despite my efforts. But Mom's box was still sealed tight as a vault. I also had support, whereas Mom did not. Sometimes I was shocked by how I could still slip into being overly concerned about either of my parents' well-being rather than my own; they could eclipse my own needs in no time.

It actually took several weeks for me to get the whole story. I did not get it from Mom. Instead, I got the details from Penny, who lived near my parents. Penny was open, always forthright whenever I asked her opinion. She was in nursing school at the time, doing a rotation at a nearby hospital in their addiction recovery unit as part of her degree requirements. She said she had stopped by my parents' home to visit for a few minutes before going to work, something she did on a regular basis. When no one came to the door, she used her key to let herself in. It appeared no one was home until she went to my parents' bedroom. As soon as she entered, she saw my dad in bed, his face beet red and sweating profusely. When he slowly looked up, he was in a stupor. Penny was shocked to see her uncle like this, and was very concerned. Realizing Mom was not home, she immediately assessed his distress, thinking he was about to have a heart attack or even a stroke. "Unc (her nickname for him), I need to get you to the emergency room as soon as possible. You don't look well at all." There was a long pause. Saying he was afraid to sit up due to his blood pressure being dangerously high, he then said what Penny could not believe. Out of his stupor he lucidly admitted: "No, honey, I need to go to a rehabilitation center. I am an alcoholic."

Penny said she was stunned by his admission. She had had

no idea he was an alcoholic. No one did, not even Dottie, Mom's dearest friend, who was in daily contact. Ours was a home like so many others: higher-functioning homes where the disease can be kept secret for years. On the outside, my parents' lives appeared stable and calm. Unlike Charlie and Alta's lives, there were not any jail sentences or messy divorces. There had not even been a DUI or serious car crash. In stark contrast to his father, Dad was passionate, being highly successful at work. There rarely had been a single defining event that screamed "alcoholic" until the recent years. Even then, it still had not been apparent to most people.

Due to Dad's surprising admission, there was no time to waste. As if by divine intervention, Penny knew where to call and who to talk with, for she was working at the very place that was perfect for my dad. Once she called, she secured a very hard-to-find bed, which had miraculously opened up at that very moment. A true miracle.

Admitted immediately, he spent two days and nights in ICU on an IV drip of valium along with other medications, while he slowly detoxified his body from the near fatal intake of alcohol. He later told me he had been away from home for a couple of days working as a consultant in the Imperial Valley. The morning he was due to drive home, he drank a fifth of gin, got in his car, driving over 200 miles (a three to four-hour drive) to get home. By some miracle, he had just gotten home when Penny came to visit.

I was breathless upon hearing this. The odds of him making it home safely in that inebriated state were practically zero. Somehow, he had. As I looked back, big miracles had coincided that day: he made it home safely, he knew he had reached bottom, he could say what he needed, and Penny was the conduit for his placement. The whole thing was just astonishing to me. I felt chills run through my body the more I considered this . . . next to the horrifying alternatives.

Six months after I sent my last letter to Dad reiterating my concerns after my Christmas visit, truly *not expecting anything to come of it*, he was now in a recovery program. A dream come true! But Dad being in such a program also brought an uncomfortable mix of feelings for me. Of course, *for years*, I had longed for all of us to be released from the grip only addiction can hold, but I did not dare hope for too much. Now, my wish had come true. Could I dare hope for anything more, like reconciliation? Even if we could reconcile, what would happen if he could not maintain sobriety? And if he did relapse, would the fall end all possibility of healing, once and for all?

Soon after my dad began his 30-day treatment program, I asked a colleague, who was a practicing psychiatrist, what he thought my dad's chances were of a sustained recovery. Given his age, at nearly 65, next to his family history, my colleague said the odds were against him, as these significant factors often cement intractable dysfunctional behaviors learned years before as well as a relentless longing for alcohol.

With this information, I knew the uncertainty of whether my dad could remain sober would put me on yet another emotional roller coaster ride. So many "what if" questions circled around in my head. What if he cannot remain sober? What if he fools himself, and us, into thinking he can drink socially? Even worse, what if he dies in the process? Knowing this, my lifeline card with the 12-step mantra *One day at a time* became my guide. It was the only way.

I knew he was in good hands. I was not so sure about Mom. She was uneasy every week when we spoke by phone. Yes, I realized her world had been turned upside down from what had become the norm for over thirty years, but instead of being hopeful, she was agitated and ungrounded. No matter how often we spoke about recovery while he was still in treatment, she was fixated on waiting for the other shoe to drop. After all, it had become the only reality she had known.

Dad's true character was put to the test. In keeping with his history of being ready to rise to a challenge, he miraculously embraced his month-long program. Not only did he let go of drinking, but he ended years of smoking, a habit he said began in his early teens. Once committed, **HE WAS ALL IN.** From start to finish, he characteristically applied himself to the AA principles. He slowly began to come to terms with some of his painful past. He told me his self-loathing and remorse was now gone. In its place, he said, came a long sought-after inner peace. I was thrilled to hear how well he was doing.

It was quite a different story for Mom. At one point, as a courtesy to Dad, she reluctantly attended a session for family members at the treatment center. She rarely opened up fully to even her closest friends, let alone strangers. This would be a huge undertaking, surrounded by all strangers except for Dad. One of the group counselors noted her reluctance to share. Later he asked if she wanted to schedule a private counseling appointment with him. I was thrilled when she agreed. I longed for her to have someone else to talk to other than me. When the appointment came and went and I did not hear from her, I knew something was wrong. I called her to inquire. My heart sunk when she sadly said, "He forgot we had the appointment." That was by far the worst thing anyone could do to Mom at this time (or any time, really; I was furious with the counselor). Mom was a very private person by nature. For this situation she had made herself vulnerable. In that instant I knew she would never forgive him. She would never give him (or anyone else) a second chance. She had been de-valued and mistreated by her own father years before, a deep, long-held wound that had now been triggered. The counselor's oversight meant she did not matter to him, that she was easily forgotten. Despite the fact the counselor called, was deeply apologetic offering to set up another appointment, it meant nothing to her. She would never take a risk like that again. Her silence meant the door to that possibility was irrevocably closed.

Even though she was very happy for Dad's newfound sobriety, frequently telling him so, she struggled with how or why she had ever been part of this problem in the first place; after all, she was not the alcoholic. Deep inside, she resented the fact that she had been subjected to it for so long; it had altered her life in every imaginable way.

Once home, Dad happily and faithfully attended AA meetings on a regular basis, finding great solace due to his new lease on life. He was passionately moving forward. Eventually, he became a leader in his AA community, sponsoring those who asked.

Again, Mom was not ready to join him. I also had reservations. For years, both of us had had to pack away a lot of feelings. As with most family members living in an alcoholic family, it was never safe to be forthright or expect too much even if or when sobriety might be in place. Too many times we had been fooled. Too many times we had been shaken to our core. Would this be another in a long line of devastating disappointments? Yes, we were very happy to see his newfound joy from being sober. I wondered if he were really ready to hear from us or would we be marginalized again.

Mom had been a casualty of all of this. It had broken my heart to see addiction's effect on her over the years. I wanted more for her now. I wanted her to break free from all that had held her back, to let go of her resentments. She would have to allow the past to speak for the first time. I wondered if she would be able (or willing). When I told her this one night she quietly listened. After a long sigh, she agreed I was probably right then quickly changed the subject. I knew this indicated she would not say much; her resolve was final. So was mine. I had to speak my truth. Something always kept moving me forward, no matter what the cost. I had a shit-load of anger mixed with resentment, to put it mildly. I had keen memories of many insulting and humiliating episodes that had transpired over the years. No matter what, I knew it was now time for me to speak.

I broached the subject with Dad one night on the phone. "I want to talk about how your drinking affected me over the years. I want to heal. I want our family to leave the past behind. Are you open to this?" By this time, Dad had been exposed to individual and group counseling in his program. He welcomed my request with enthusiasm. To me, it was ironic that he rarely appreciated what I did as a counselor and psychologist before he was sober; he would usually blow me off if I ever brought up the subject. But now, he thought counseling was the best thing ever. (That was so like him to think he was the first person to ever experience this.) I appreciated his newfound readiness. Knowing I did not want to lead with accusations, I carefully selected some of my experiences to share, being cautious not to enter into the blame game. One of the many benefits of my own counseling was having a safe place to vent my feelings, no matter how toxic they were. It was also the right place to explore what I might say to Dad before having the conversation.

Month after month, either by phone or in letters, I touched on a variety of issues: how I had felt forced to live in secrecy; how I had felt compelled to protect our family's image; my fear that he would endanger himself as well as others while driving drunk; my anger that he could have lost his business sooner. I ended by sharing my despair when another birthday or holiday was ruined. "Dad, I think alcoholism was really a spirit-stealer. I think we have all been robbed by the disease, finding it difficult for love to even find the light of day." He appreciated my insights. Eventually, he let himself realize how this disease had also been a "spirit-stealer" to him in his childhood years, something I had only guessed at, at the time. He even began to see the bigger picture of alcoholism's grip on several generations of our family. The legacy had been passed on in silence until now.

I felt our hearts begin to open to one another. I longed for love to be the center of our relationship once again. But could it? My thoughts told me I was now ready to move on, but my dreams told me otherwise. They alerted me to even deeper-seated feelings. Repeatedly, I dreamt of being excited to see him, now that he was in recovery, only to find him drunk and/or still smoking. This recurring theme sharply focused my attention to the anger I felt due to the cumulative betrayal resulting in the despair I had experienced before he became sober. Weekly professional help allowed me to address this, along with my many memories of disappointment and abandonment, knowing it was all a part of healing my heart.

In time, I slowly began to trust my dad's commitment to his sobriety due to his consistent willingness to talk openly and honestly. No longer was he deceptive, leaving out critical information, as in the past. Rarely, if ever, did I have to search for what was not being said, for he had deeply accepted all had happened in his life. He was emotionally honest for the first time in a long time. He accepted the dark underbelly of the life he had tried to silence through drinking. Most importantly, he felt deeply grateful for his newfound relationship with his "Higher Power," as he referred to it.

A few months after his treatment program ended he showed me a letter he had written to himself before leaving treatment. All of the participants were asked to answer six questions, which would be mailed to them a month later. Here is what my dad wrote:

What I learned about myself? My self-esteem has been restored. I don't feel guilty anymore. The need for people in my life is important to me. In the beginning, I thought sharing in a group would be difficult. I found no reticence in doing so. I am proud that surrender came to me. I feel clean.

What did I learn about the disease? It is a powerful master. If not confronted and dealt with, the result is death before I'm ready. It completely ruins one's life, loved ones, friends, work performance, health. It is diabolical, but can be conquered by following the 12 steps of AA and dedicating yourself to one day at a time.

My future? Looks good. I have no qualms about handling it, providing that I follow the 12 steps and work with AA.

How do I feel about recovery? I feel great physically, mentally and spiritually.

How do I feel about myself and the program? I bought the whole package with an open mind and was impressed with the quality and comprehensive approach.

My message for myself? Now that I have this education about alcohol and me, the ball is in my court to handle. With the realization that I can't do it alone, I will reach out for help.

Now that, once again, I have contact with my Higher Power, I feel relieved. No longer do I have to carry the burdens by myself.

- Stay away from stress-producing areas. Do not brood by yourself or indulge in self-pity.
- Seek people to talk with and be with.
- Seek new and interesting hobbies; reinforce and be more active in established activities such as exercise, golf, gardening, etc.
- Stay close and appreciate the constant wonders of nature. Be a part of it.
- Never again lose contact with your Highest Power.

Reading his answers brought me new insights. Mom felt that same way. Every little bit that he shared allowed me to see more of him. However, It was a letter he sent to me a year and a half later that brought me to tears. He began by saying:

"For the first time in many years I got a flu bug that liked me a lot. That feeling wasn't reciprocated. Now the fever has gone and I feel almost whole again."

He went on, saying:

"What I want to relate to you is my appreciation for your standing by me, trying to reach me, not succeeding, and trying again and again. I now know what you and Mom went through, though I didn't really appreciate the interference at the time. My attitude then was, 'this is my life and I'll run it any damn way I want.' An alcoholic doesn't seem to care what he does to himself. What he doesn't know is how his behavior affects those close to him. He can't see that he is turning off those close to him and blames them for their stupid behavior. He never blames himself.

There were times when I embarrassed you. For doing that I am truly sorry. Certainly, it was never with intent. My father did the same to me and couldn't believe he did when faced with it. Those episodes are hard to forget. Long ago I forgave him, but forgetting is something else.

You and I have a wonderful, close, father-daughter relationship. This love affair has been going on for a long, long time. Soul mates? Yes, I think we are.

Thanks to you, Mom and Penny, et al., I have a new life extension. Every day is a wonderful day, exciting yet comfortable. I'm at peace, having fun, enjoying. I'm not struggling uphill anymore. Everything I do seems to be easy and turns out so well. AA has been a big factor. It is truly amazing the number of people involved and the great good it does. It is a blueprint for living that everyone can use.

So, your father wants to say 'thanks' with love. I'm sure happy that we have a loving relationship and can share at least part of our lives together.

Much love,

Dad"

For the first time in a very long time, I began to feel valued. I felt his heart open, making it more possible to feel seen and heard. He was unwavering about what mattered most: sobriety, support of family, and love. Even though he wrote in his WW II diary years before that his definition of success was living a happy, full and complete life, he left out the fact he mistakenly thought alcohol was part of that equation. Now, he knew the truth: he did not need alcohol as a way to find camaraderie or to relax, or as a medication or a way to shut down retreating from the unfinished emotional pain of the past. Being close to death had forced him to surrender. As a result, he was reunited with the guiding presence of Spirit, his Higher Power.

Until this moment, my many tears had been not only about feeling deeply angry, but also helpless due to alcoholism being the "elephant in the room." Now I wept tears of pure joy, feeling a profound sense of gratitude. It was finally safe for our hearts to remain open. Now, our long-needed healing could begin, allowing love to find its way back to our family. That, by far, was the biggest miracle of all.

I attended Al-Anon meetings even after Dad's recovery was well in place for I knew, as he did, it was a commitment to a life-long process. While at Al-Anon meetings, I noted my appreciation for the simple presence of everyone there: for their strength; for their pain in loving an alcoholic; for their honesty. They were truly some of the most courageous people with whom I ever had the honor of being. For that, I owed a deep debt of gratitude to each one. They gave me the strength to find my way through the darkness of my own emotional pain…eventually finding the light.

A very happy time for Mom, Dad and Dottie with
Dad firmly committed to sobriety.

Note: Addiction plagues my family and extended family to this day. I have had several aunts, uncles, first and second cousins on both sides of my family sadly affected by ongoing drug and alcohol abuse. In some instances it has led to premature death. I, luckily, have not experienced a pull toward addiction in this way. The taste of alcohol does not appeal to me, nor does the effect. Some doctors say I did not inherit the enzyme pattern usually associated with alcoholism. This may be true. However, I credit Mom for being a steady force in many important ways. She drank moderately. We always ate sensibly. It may seem odd to say, but we had a comforting routine in our home despite Dad's drinking. The effect of addiction pulled me more toward over-functioning. I was a workaholic. I could be compulsive. I would experience bouts of low-grade depression, on the one hand, and anxiety on the other. Al-Anon principles help me to this day. Understanding ways in which I can be co-dependent also helps. Following a healthy lifestyle (mind, body and spirit) has been a top priority. Rarely does a week go by when I don't remember that I, too, am in recovery. I am in recovery from the many ways addiction affected me.

THE
POWER OF
TRANSITIONS

Chapter 9

An Untimely Death

D ad's commitment to sobriety never wavered. He was open to everyone about his recovery by making it clear he had no problem with anyone around him who wanted to drink socially. In many ways, my parents were able to return to the things they enjoyed together. Playing golf, entertaining friends in addition to traveling became their priorities. They had always had fun together in their earlier years. They were avid readers and doers of crossword puzzles. They had an easy-going camaraderie on many intellectual matters. Now, I saw that return. Never did I know what Mom chose to share about her experience living with him as an active alcoholic. I did not know if she ever shared her numerous fears or frustrations. Maybe their 39-year marriage formed the basis to usher in a quieter way to make peace with what happened. Clearly, she was happy for him in his newfound sobriety. She usually told me this in our weekly phone conversations. It was sweet to hear.

What was even sweeter for me was *I had my dad back*. Every time we talked, we slowly healed. He was open to seeing the effect of his past. Both of his parents, along with his paternal grandfather, were alcoholics. He fully grasped his genetic predisposition toward the disease. Family dynamics had sowed the seeds for chaos, instability and abuse. He saw how alcohol was central to him "having fun" as a temporary mask for anything he did not want to deal with. He realized how much emotional pain he had carried by pushing it away. Originally, he, like many others, had thought the skid row bum was the only definition of a "real" drunk. Now, he knew they were a mere fraction of those who are alcoholics. The time he grew up in viewed alcoholism as a moral failing, a crime, even a sin; it certainly was not known as a medical condition. Now, he knew otherwise. I saw that as much as he loved his work and golf, his obsessive approach to both had set him up to eventually need alcohol in his life. His deep-seated emotional pain left unattended became expressed through his driven, compulsive nature. His use of alcohol as an anesthesia made sense: it was legal, it was fast-acting and it was easy.

Alcoholism can happen to such good people. My dad was no exception. Neither were his parents. I think alcohol might have played less of a role for Dad's parents in their later years. It seemed that Charlie had been able to make things right as best he could. Dad always appreciated what little financial help Charlie had been able to provide while in college. Charlie truly wanted to see him succeed. My dad later respected his father's adoption of better values, values he said his dad learned from some of his Mormon neighbors over the years. Charlie now comes to me asking if he can offer his insights from spirit. I am thrilled that he wants to for he was a man I had never met. And the little I heard about him was not favorable. *"I had the soul of a poet. I loved to read, to imagine life at another time. Much of the reality of my life didn't fit with my true nature. I spent many years lost, drinking, and womanizing. It just made matters worse. I was grateful my family still accepted me after all I had put them through. I began to adopt better values before I died."*

Alta tried, too. Not long after her last husband died (she had outlived all four, three of whom had been younger), she was no longer able to live alone. Both Dad and Herb helped move her from California to Washington State to live with their oldest sister Muriel and her husband. When they closed out her bank account they realized she only had $250 to her name. In keeping with Alta's true nature though, she had thought that was plenty on which to live. She had lived in a vastly different reality most of the time. Eventually, when her health issues became more advanced, she spent the last few years of her life in a care facility, living near my aunt. My dad and his siblings came together when it was most needed, contributing what they could to offset the cost.

One day, I received a handwritten letter from Alta. The letter came as a complete surprise, as I had not had any contact with her since she had been to my family's home for that fateful dinner fifteen years prior. In her newsy letter, she not only talked about where she was in addition to what she was doing, but actually asked how I was doing—quite a departure from her self-centered behavior. For the first time, I began to feel a connection to her, especially noting that, at the end, the letter was signed, *"Grandma."* The letter was certainly fortuitous, because four months later, at the age of 83, she passed away. This letter might have been her last. I now ask her to share more. *"Yes, this was my way to reach out to you, to make peace with my past which*

sadly didn't include you much. I looked for love in many of the wrong places. I felt
unworthy of anything good. Alcohol made it impossible to live in a meaningful way.
I have such love for you as one of my grandchildren. I wanted you to know this."
I was touched to hear these words. At last, I could understand how
her many challenges prohibited her from living a better life. For the
first time I could feel her love. Finally, after all these years, I could
feel proud to call her my Grandma.

My family's newfound peace moved us forward in our lives. For
me, moving forward brought a new marriage along with two wonderful
stepsons who we saw regularly. My new husband, Ken, brought a lively
energy to my life along with an unquenchable sense of adventure. In
spite of being more adept in the world of engineering and business,
he appreciated my interest in the inner world of psychology. My
stepsons, aged six and ten at the time, added great fun. This time
also brought an eventual return to graduate school for me, being in
my mid-30s, to study more in psychology. Not always liking to be a
student in a prescribed program for very long, I dreamed of working
in more depth with those who wanted deeper healing. I was primed
to do whatever I could to further my training.

It was a happy time in every way. Christmas brought my family
together in an entirely different fashion, one based in sobriety. Ken and
I had a wonderful time celebrating the season with my parents. For the
first time in years, I actually looked forward to being together. What
a dramatic contrast from the year before when Dad had broken his
promise of abstinence during my holiday visit. When I had shortened
my visit to return home prematurely, I had never dreamt we would
be together again. Except perhaps for a funeral … his. Now the
situation had reversed. We were, at long last, happily together. Not

only was Dad sober, I also noticed Mom had softened. It seemed like a weight had been lifted from her shoulders, for she could trust Dad's commitment to sobriety. As my dad drove us to the airport to return home, Ken sat in the front seat with him while Mom and I sat together in the back. Once we finished talking, she reached for my hand...a very rare gesture for her. At first, I felt a bit awkward, not knowing what to think, but once I let go of my reticence, I was able to truly receive her love. For a long moment, she caressed my fingers in hers in silence. I felt this touching gesture was her way to say how much she appreciated having our family back. Her touch erased the years of frustration I had carried at rarely being able to please her. I had struggled as far back as childhood wanting to fix things so she would be happy. This unexpected expression was a watershed moment for me. With all we had been through, now for the first time, we could be free of the past. Now we could simply be mother and daughter. No further words were said until we reached the airport. Her gesture had spoken deeply. Something had opened between us, healing my long-held resentment about her previous emotional distance.

~⁀)

"I had this dream last night," Mom said one morning after breakfast. "I want to tell you about it." My parents had come to Oregon the following summer to visit for a few weeks, staying at the treasured beach apartment they had once owned. Of course, I was very interested in hearing her dream; it offered a chance to know her in a deeper way. "In this dream, I'm walking on a beach. In the distance, I see a house built on stilts that looks interesting. Once I reach it, I climb up the long outdoor staircase, open the door and go in. I'm shocked to realize the one-room house is completely empty, void of furniture, people or even objects. It's just bare." At that point, I asked how she felt.

"I'm anxious," she said, "I want to leave. I turn around to go out the door I came in, but I realize it's now gone. There is no way out. I'm trapped inside." The dream had abruptly ended at that moment with her still feeling very unsettled. She wondered what this meant.

I offered this: "Just six months ago you seemed relaxed and happy. What has changed?"

"I envy your father's deep sense of peace now that's he's sober. I wish I felt the same way. I thought I would in time, but I don't."

"You felt trapped by Dad's drinking for years," I suggested. "Maybe this dream is showing you what that looked like? This could be an opening for you. This could help you heal, to find a better way. Let's replay the dream creating a new scenario. Maybe you won't feel trapped any longer."

However, once I spoke, her eyes became vacant. I realized that she had not heard most of what I said. Something had told her there was no use in further examination. In her learned reaction to Dad's drinking, she had shut down to any possibilities. After a long silence, she said, "Oh, it doesn't matter, really. It is what it is."

I had no idea this dream would foreshadow the *untimely* end to Mom's life. But two months later, she was gone. The news sent shockwaves through every cell of my body upon Ken's delivery of the sad news. How could this be true? This had to be a mistake. I flashed back to her many years of healthy exercise; she had been one of the few women in town to join a gym, working with a personal trainer. She had played golf regularly and had rarely missed her morning walk beforehand. She had always been ahead of the curve when it came to healthy eating. Except for an acute episode of colitis at the height of Dad's drinking plus an occasional cigarette, yearly check-ups at her doctor visits had never revealed anything of consequence. Yet she was gone, just like that: it was simply beyond my comprehension. The suddenness left me frozen in place, unable to move. Tears gushed. I could hardly catch my breath, as Ken held me, allowing the first wave of shock to subside. Once able, I called Dad. He was bereft. Bewildered. "Dad, what in the world happened," I asked, still in disbelief. He could barely answer my question. All I heard was, "In the hospital, late night call, heart attack." I attempted to get more information, but it was useless. He was trying to make sense of what happened and could not; he was in shock.

Ken had already purchased an airline ticket for me so I could leave the next morning. I made arrangements with my fellow graduate students to keep me posted about the monumental classwork I would miss; they later informed each of my professors about my absence as I hastily left in a daze.

Once with Dad, and my godmother, Dottie, the story began to take shape. Between the two of them I learned that Mom had not felt well the day before. She had returned home from playing golf, ate lunch, then rested (her usual routine). When she woke she did not feel at all well.

I interjected, "But Dad, what were her symptoms?"

He muttered, "Oh, some kind of stomach upset, I guess."

"You guess? What does that mean?"

After a struggle to find the words he finally said, "With her symptoms, Dottie and I decided to take her to the hospital."

"You took her to the hospital the day before she died, never telling me?" I was incredulous. He brushed past my question. Already I was thinking Mom's symptoms had to have been more than just a stomach upset. Otherwise, they would never have gone to the hospital. To include Dottie (well-versed in medical knowledge and a volunteer at the hospital) meant something of a more serious nature had happened.

"The tests revealed that she had had a mild heart attack," he said. "They suggested she stay overnight for further observation."

Wow, I noted silently, Mom had not liked hospitals, or many doctors for that matter. I could only imagine how anxious she must have felt. Then, it hit me...I could have talked with her that night, IF I had even known she was in the hospital. My head spinning, I took another deep breath. "When did she die? "

"Late that night," Dad revealed, "The backside of her heart exploded. Everyone was shocked, especially her doctors."

Even knowing more of the story, I could not stop wondering why Dad had waited until the middle of the next day to call. He had known hours before. He could have called, even in the middle of the night, but he did not. I could not let go of this question. It put me back in a mindset I was familiar with from his alcoholic days when I had learned to be vigilant about what was not being said or done. My emerging sense of wariness would soon have reason to fully take hold.

As if the late news of Mom's untimely death were not enough for me to grasp, I was shocked to learn Dad had had Mom's body cremated before I even arrived at their home. Only 24 hours had elapsed from the time I learned of her death upon my arrival to Southern California. I was livid and, at the same time, heartbroken. I would never be able to see Mom again. I would never be able to say goodbye. My dad did not talk with anyone: not me, Penny or Dottie. It never occurred to him that we might want to see her one last time to say goodbye. It was a one-two punch for me: first Mom was suddenly dead; secondly, it was now impossible for me see her. I slowly began to see a callous, cold side to my dad. Had it always been there, I wondered? Or, was I seeing this for the first time? Anger filled my voice as tears ran down my face. I confronted him, saying: "Why in the world didn't you talk to me before making arrangements for Mom's body? Did you think it didn't matter to me or that I didn't want to be part of the discussion?"

Looking nonplussed, he simply said: "I didn't think it mattered to you."

Desperately trying to grasp what he just said, contempt overruled: "How could you possibly think that? She was my mother, for God's sake!"

Gone was any semblance of partnership in our newfound father-daughter alliance. His actions left me reeling. Still, there was more to come. I discovered he had already made plans for her memorial service, asking a minister who did not even know Mom to do the service. It was so impersonal. I had had no say in any of it. I was in utter disbelief, stunned by the likes of another all-too-familiar type of betrayal that I had thought to be in the past.

In that moment, to say I could not understand my dad's actions was an understatement: they were seriously beyond comprehension. But I was not going to be silenced or confused as I had been in the early days of his drinking; I was going to get to the bottom of this before our relationship suffered any more damage. Somehow, I found a source of courage—from where I had no idea—allowing me to find the right words. As our conversation progressed, I did not let him off the hook. He eventually admitted how utterly lost he felt by her sudden death.

"Honey, I was used to taking charge of any crisis from a very early age. It ended the chaos. It's second nature to me." He needed to feel in control, he said.

"Did it ever occur to you that we could have talked about this together," I said, sounding perplexed.

"No, it never occurred to me to include you or anyone else for that matter; I just saw it being my sole responsibility."

That was a very familiar belief for me, as well. I had felt alone in carrying the burden of responsibility for my family's circumstances until I had learned differently in Al-Anon. With his insights, a shift began to occur. We began to find a mutual way through this crisis. Later, as I looked back at that moment, I felt sad for both of us. I realized the obvious: the legacy of alcoholism had been passed on to two more generations of our family. Now, I *fully* realized what it meant for both of us to come from alcoholic homes: early on we had assumed an unusual amount of responsibility; we established a belief around the unavailability of outside support. We needed to handle everything independently.

A big hurdle now behind us, day-by-day, we tenuously began to build a new understanding. I stayed for three weeks to help with what comes after a loved one dies. But, I held off stating my biggest concern until the time was right. One night as he sat on the edge of his bed holding his head in his hands, I waited for his tears to finish. He was grieving the loss of life as he knew it. He would have to move forward at some point, he said. As I prepared to address my concern, I took a deep breath. As I exhaled I finally said: "You and Mom were married 42 years. Her death is a huge shock for all of us, so unexpected and untimely. Knowing that, will you remain in recovery as you move forward or will this threaten your three years of sobriety, especially since your interest in AA meetings has waned?"

His voice never wavered: "No, honey, I will be fine. I'm no longer interested in attending AA meetings if the point of the meeting revolves around others telling their worst experiences being drunk, over and over again. I want to be with people who are ready and willing to move forward in a positive way." The depth of his truth resonated in me. I knew I could trust his resolve.

While flying home I tried to process the past three weeks, but could not. I was in a daze from the shock of it all. All I knew was Mom was gone, I was 39 years old, and I faced my hardest semester of graduate school. Wondering how I could possibly go on, my anxiety heightened. My mind frantically searched for solutions. When none appeared, my anxiety grew worse. Gradually, the grasping for options that did not exist exhausted me. Overwhelmed, I was forced to let go. As I let out a deep, gut-wrenching sigh of resignation, I felt a presence, like never before, surround me in peace telling me that ALL would be OK. I needed to trust ALL was in Divine Right Order. Instantly, for no logical reason, I felt protected in spite of all that had happened. As I took this quality of peace within, the next message came: *"You are now ready to learn a better way of being in your life, one that requires being more open to accepting the moment, no matter how devastating it might be. You will learn to trust the darkness...and the unknown."*

I felt held in this altered state of mind for the entire trip home. The messages resonated deeply in me. never warranting further analysis. I felt an unshakeable trust that everything before me would find resolution in its own way. Months later, as I looked back on this moment I saw that death, like alcoholism, had now become my new teacher.

Regardless of the coursework demands of the second year of my doctoral program, I immersed myself in reading everything I could about the grief process. I immediately realized I, like many, lived in a society conditioned to deny death. As a result, I knew few ways to cope with it now that it was my reality. What I had witnessed in my family, as well as in other families over the years, was my only blueprint: death was inevitably sad, and viewed as something to endure in silence.

Something told me there had to be a different way of living with death; I was determined not to exist in grief the rest of my life. I immersed myself in reading what was available, looking for a better way to understand this inevitable transition.

My Christian upbringing had remained part of my religious foundation. But as I read various books written about death from a religious perspective, I was dissatisfied. The many questions I had went unanswered. One of the most compelling questions I wanted to understand was what had happened to me on the plane as I flew home after Mom's death? Who or what had been speaking to me? Was it real? My skepticism could not outweigh the undeniable power. The sense of protection and peace remained throughout the numerous challenges that school and family presented. Expanding my search, I began to read more from a spiritual and metaphysical perspective. This exposure provided me with a more encompassing view. It gave me a philosophy about death, as well as the otherworldly things that can happen. In time, I realized the best way to describe what had happened was I had *simply and profoundly been touched by an energy that I called Spirit*. Grace had eased its way through my grief, showing me the power of trust and surrender. Through surrender I was learning to navigate the unknown.

I worked to be as present as I could with my grief. I journaled. I wrote letters to Mom in spirit. I talked to Dad. I shared with Ken and friends. I read. I cried. I sat in nature. In my lowest moments, I talked to Dottie.

Long ago, my parents had chosen their closest friends, Dottie and Wickie, to be my legal guardians and godparents. They had been godparents in the truest sense. I had felt adored by them, whether they were visiting us or I was spending weekends with them. When I spent a weekend with them, Wickie, being a master carpenter, had always made me something special, be it a stool to sit on while he worked on other projects or a ladder for my parakeet to climb, or a box to hold my treasures. Each morning of my stay, Dottie had always had a secret gift for me to find. Visiting the local zoo had been an all-time favorite for both me and Wickie; we had spent hours there, seeing every animal while he documented all we did with his fancy camera. Even though Wickie had sadly died prematurely when I was 10, Dottie had not only been Mom's closest friend, but had eventually become a surrogate mother to me. My parents' return to living next door to her (just as they had during WW II) was a testament to their deep love for one another.

Dottie's openness in our talks was refreshing. Her emotional honesty was a relief to experience, as she revealed her own feelings about Mom's sudden death. She was openly grieving the death of her closest friend; I was grieving the death of my mom. More importantly, we were doing it together. It was her presence that constantly soothed my aching heart. Her insights helped me make sense of what my dad was not able to process. I found I could ask her anything. Her answers were always shared in a thoughtful. loving manner. As much as I loved Mom, she rarely, if ever, was forthcoming with matters close to her heart. I usually had had to wait for the right moment, or keep after her to answer my more sensitive questions. Even then, she had chosen not to reveal much. Not so with Dottie. It was not long before our occasional calls to one another became weekly conversations we both treasured. Even though I felt devastated by Mom's death and longed for a different reality, now something larger was at work. Dottie brought an ongoing maternal connection to my life that would help steady my emotional footing for many years to come. Dottie now says from spirit, *"I felt so sad for you, losing your mother the way you did. I no longer had my closest dearest friend nearby. Somehow we were meant to be together in this way, but for the longest time, I could not see why. In time, I saw a bigger picture. I knew you knew, too, even though we didn't talk about it. I was meant to fill in for your mom from this moment on; it had been our soul agreement."*

My dear Dottie, a godmother in the truest sense.

My deep connection to Dottie could not have come a moment too soon for, once again, I saw another side of Dad that was hard to bear. One night not long after I had returned home we were on the phone together. I broached a delicate subject: "Dad, what do you think we should do with Mom's ashes?" His long pause was disturbing. I felt my stomach sink. When he did not reply immediately, I knew something was amiss.

"Hey, why the silence? This seems to be the next thing we need to discuss."

Then, in a matter-of-fact tone he said something I will never forget: "I have already dealt with that. I gave her ashes to a fishing boat crew at the harbor to disperse with as they saw fit."

I screamed silently, in total disbelief, my head spinning. I tried to regain my focus, but could not. I started sobbing uncontrollably, unable to catch my breath. He knew something was *very* wrong and was clueless as to what it was. This moment felt chillingly similar to what he had done after Mom died—again, being insensitive to what I might have been wanting or even what Mom would have wanted. It was happening all over again! Even though he was now sober, he had behaved like he had in the past, like a total jerk, a true "assaholic." I realized I had more of my dad back than I had wanted.

This time, I had no willingness to understand his position, no energy to mediate. Once I somehow regained my balance, I made sure he knew how I felt. "I have NO words to tell you how angry I am that you have betrayed me, once again. You've left me out. You've stripped me of having any voice about how to handle the dispersal of Mom's ashes. Something very dear to my heart. How could you be so insensitive?"

His voice was uneasy being quite contrite; he knew he had messed up. Lamely, he added, "I didn't know what else to do."

In this moment I realized I was done. Any further talk was futile. He was not remotely capable of understanding my position. I hurt so much that my heart, once again, went underground, sealing itself off from further injury.

Once my dad entered recovery, I had thought I had him back in every way. He had been open to understanding his past—how it affected his behavior, us, and our family. Wounds had been healing between us. Now, however, any future healing came to a screeching halt. I could not fool myself any longer. I realized I was seeing more of him than I cared to see. I did not have a clue how to manage it. What I did know was I had a sober dad who I could not trust not to betray me at any given time. Continuing to open my heart to this man was dangerous. It was way too threatening to even consider.

Chapter 10

A Threatening Diagnosis

I knew I had to face the ugliness of what I saw in my dad's behavior, but the pain of doing so was unbearable. The man I was so crazy about as a child had serious flaws. Part of me did not want to admit it. I wanted him to be my dad, free of any imperfections. I sat with the pain of this for weeks, not knowing how to move forward. Over time, as I addressed his failings I saw how futile it was to blame him: he, like all of us, was simply human. As much as he said he understood his past, he was still held by some of it. The disappointing truth was he was very self-centered. He truly could often be thoughtless and insensitive, going to great lengths to avoid any emotional pain. He wanted what he wanted, failing to see how this would affect anyone else. As a result, it was easy for me to feel not only marginalized or even invisible, but also deeply rejected. With this stark truth now in full view, I took a giant step back from our relationship. Having seen how I had been pricked by the many thorns that had come with our love, I wanted no more.

Our conversations were occasional and brief. My guard was up no matter what we talked about. Whether I spoke or listened, I was detached. This was a trying time, being only a few months after Mom passed. Naturally, I wanted to support him (once again, I realized how this was so much a part of my co-dependent nature), but I also knew where I needed to place my personal boundaries in order to feel safe. Dad really did not know how to be supportive to anyone. He had relied on Mom to fill that need for him. She had been there for him, listening or advising, as needed. She had been his confidante. I wondered if she had ever felt his support in the same way. I could move into filling that role, but I refused. It would be a long time before we could ever re-visit the emotional pain inflicted over the issue of Mom's ashes or anything else related to her death. The subject remained too raw for me.

I knew Dad would not remain single for long; he was extroverted, always loving to share his life with someone special. He stayed living in the condo he shared with Mom at their retirement community. Six months later after Mom's passing he told me he was now part of the "casserole brigade," receiving food from many of the single women living in his neighborhood. It made sense that he would be sought after: he was widowed, in good health, fun, and energetic. It was easy to find him attractive. However, I was not sure what to think. After all, he was still my dad. However, I had to get used to him being my dad being pursued by other women. Whether he dated or not, I had learned to be far more invested in my life than his. I knew he would do what he wanted regardless of my opinion.

One night, I listened to him briefly share about the women he dated. I stayed detached as he described each one. One was a retired actress (who I later met). I think he was flattered by the attention, being attracted to her beauty. The second woman was very pushy (I thought), being quite adept at manipulating men; she wanted to marry my dad in the worst way. He liked her because she was fun-loving and could dance well. I was told by Dottie that she had a reputation of getting what she wanted. She even called me once, saying how much she wanted us to be a family. I was repulsed by her pushiness. With her in his life, I was definitely concerned. When I told him that, he just laughed. He said he knew about her possessiveness, never taking it seriously. I hoped that was the case.

Living 1000 miles away from Dad provided me the distance I needed. Our conversations felt surreal. I felt an obligation to listen because he was my dad, although once again, my heart was estranged. It was a foregone conclusion that he was going to remarry. I left it at that.

A little over a year after Mom died, Dad found the right person in Corrine. They shared many of the same interests in addition to her having previously been a golf partner and friend of Mom's. Before they decided to marry, she asked me about Dad's commitment to sobriety. Having been previously married to an alcoholic alerted her to the potential danger she might be walking into, but it was also her training as a certified alcohol counselor that led her to be upfront about her concerns. I shared what he had said to me after Mom died: no matter what, his commitment to sobriety was unwavering. It had been as far as I knew. I encouraged her to keep talking with him about her concerns, trusting her impressions. I liked her. She was open and honest, easily talking about most anything.

By the time Dad and Corrine married two years later, I had accepted an internship at the University of California, San Diego, being one of the older interns at age 38. Once we moved to San Diego, we lived within driving distance to Dad and Corrine. Always capable, Ken put his multi-faceted business and engineering background to work finding employment while I began my year-long internship. We were able to visit Corrine and Dad when we could, but the greatest advantage was being closer to Dottie.

I was happy for Dad; however, I kept emotionally distant. Immediately, he wanted us to visit with Corrine and her two adult children. This arrangement was fine for Ken and I until my older stepson chose to leave Oregon to live with us six months after our move. The forging of this new relationship was something I protected, and I was reluctant to subject him to anything more, knowing the instability from which he had come. I told Dad we would take our time as a family, deciding when it was best to include my stepson. Dad respected my position on the matter, but I could tell by his puzzled reaction that he really did not understand it. I did not care. I was firm, offering no further explanation.

I did not question Dad's decision to remarry. I did not question the fact I never had closure about Mom's ashes. What was done, was done, as he often said. This time, I adopted the same approach. He marched forward with little interest in attending to that which was messy or required personal insight or reflection. Suppression was his middle name. This always left me with an uneasy undercurrent of anxiety. I was sensitive to seeing what he could not see, just as I had been as a child. I did not want to be blindsided by how it might impact me. Being in the profession I was helped me find a better way.

But little of the insights I shared with him about his life, or mine, for that matter, seemed of interest. As long as he could be active in his life doing what he loved, the less he attended to anything else.

Once I completed my degree, I was thrilled to be hired at the University of San Diego as a staff psychologist. By this time my younger stepson had joined our family, keeping us busy with all that goes into co-parenting two budding teenagers. Despite acquiring an instant full-time family, I would not have traded it for anything. As parents, we were quite compatible, doing all we could to provide for them. In addition, I always appreciated my colleagues who created a wonderful camaraderie in which to work and thrive; they valued emotional honesty as much as I did. It was an ideal fit for me.

But change was in the wind. Three years into his marriage to Corrine, Dad began to have urination problems. He consulted his doctor. After the exam plus test results, he got the news: *prostate cancer*. I sat in silence as he shared this. No one wanted to hear the word "cancer," especially since Dad's three siblings had, by now, died of various types of cancer. Oddly, he appeared calm as his doctor laid out the recommended treatment plan: surgery followed by radiation. Most prostate cancers were slow-growing making them fairly easy to treat; the oncologist was optimistic. So was Dad. But I was not. His brother had died from a virulent form of prostate cancer just two years previously; it was in the family. I was not about to trust anyone's optimism.

I had been used to getting off one speeding train and getting onto another most of my life. This time was no different. Dad's cancer diagnosis struck like a bullet train. The impact signaled the need for a sharper awareness of all that was threatened. Even with the unfinished business I still had with my dad, I decided it was a time for hope. It was a time for holding out for the best possible outcome. I suspended my irritation around the messiness of the past, suiting up for this new threat.

Knowing our future was now defined by a cancer diagnosis, and that I might be preparing to say goodbye to my dad, I knew I needed more emotional support. Luckily, I had kept seeing my therapist, Dr. Jan Berlin, since preparing for my doctoral dissertation a few years prior. Now, my focus turned to preparing for the next chapter with my dad. In spite of the huge ups and downs we had weathered, I did not want anything to weaken the possibility of a positive outcome. I trusted the pieces of this crazy puzzle would somehow come together.

Facing such uncertainty was *daunting*, to say the least. It was an emotional roller coaster ride on any given day. My mood went up and down as my mind constantly bombarded me with what-if questions: What if the treatment does not work? What if he does not have long to live? What if we do not have enough time together to heal our relationship?

Feeling comforted by a plan made it easier for my dad to follow the recommendations of his oncologist. He had surgery followed by radiation. Once his treatment ended he continued being active. He said he was confident that the advancements in treatment would help him remain healthy. Once again, he expressed little emotion in my presence about his diagnosis. True to his nature, he soldiered on. I, however, still had my doubts. I felt the bedrock of my very foundation shifting. It had been four years since Mom's passing. Was I being prepared for another profound loss? Ironically enough, I was, and Dad knew it, too. A letter Corrine gave to me after my dad's passing alerted me to how he underplayed his true feelings about his prognosis to me. One year after his diagnosis and treatment he wrote to her saying: *"To my loving wife, Corrine, I am truly sorry we didn't have more years together. The ones we had were great. We have enjoyed each other with love from the beginning. Upon my death I want to be cremated. If you wish a memorial service it is your choice. What you do with my ashes is no big thing, whatever is simple. The days of living are important, not the cares of death. Love, Cliff."*

In spite of ALL we had been through—his betrayals, insensitivities, and self-centeredness—the first three years of living with Dad's cancer ushered in a heightened awareness between us as father and daughter. It was time to face things head-on. Overcoming the messiness of the past, he began to live more consciously and caringly. So did I. No longer needing validation from him (thank goodness for therapy), I spoke more openly about my feelings. I hugged him more. I did not let things fester. I did not let his silence about difficult subjects become my silence. I spoke up when I needed to. I immersed myself in reading recommendations from Jan. There now was more available on the subject of conscious living and conscious dying. If Dad's death were to be the final outcome, I was even more determined not to follow the cultural script of denying its presence or believing it would lead to endless suffering. I had refused to follow that script after Mom's sudden death. I was even more determined to grow from whatever this experience brought. I never wavered with my commitment. It just seemed to rise up from within and take hold.

Making a commitment to honesty and openness could be challenging, leaving me speechless at times. This happened as my next birthday approached. A couple of weeks prior, I called Dad, asking him to join Ken and I for dinner, never thinking he would not be interested. Once I told him of our plans, he said in a cavalier tone, "Sorry, honey, but we've got a golf match and dinner planned instead." Not waiting for my response, he merrily went on to talk about something else, never returning to the subject of my invitation. I was seething with irritation due to his thoughtlessness. *It's not like he can't play golf any day of the week. I have one birthday a year. Instead he chooses this day to do what he could do any other day of the year. How many children does he have, anyway?* I had thought these moments were over. Obviously they were not. Once again, I could be caught off-guard by his dismissiveness. It would silence me, stopping me in my tracks. Absent of any further conversation, I just hung up the phone. Corrine was furious with my dad once she found out. A few days later, she made him call me to reschedule. We did find another time to get together, but I could not bring myself to speak of the incident any further.

Suddenly, Dad started experiencing intense discomfort in his back. A painful bone biopsy revealed the cancer had metastasized to the bones. His prognosis for ongoing remission was poor. Prostate cancer had been our first wake-up call. Now, we were faced with another that was several orders of magnitude higher. In line with my inner reservations about his prognosis, this reality was confirming my worst fear.

Not long after receiving this news, while still in the hospital, the parting advice to Dad from one oncologist was: *"Don't buy any green bananas!"* This was his (insensitive) way of telling my dad that he did not have long to live. I could not believe his callousness, especially as a doctor. But I put my anger aside for the moment; I had to. Clearly, more important to me was Dad's well-being.

It was a defining moment. I sat on the edge of his hospital bed, barely able to breathe. We were reeling not only from receiving the bone biopsy results, but from the pronounced prognosis made by the very inept doctor. Dad had tears in his eyes, as did I, for we both knew this was the beginning of the end. No longer could he remain steadfast in his belief that everything would be fine as long as he followed a doctor's plan. Now, there was no plan.

He had never discussed his worries or fears with me (even though his letter to Corrine a year after the initial diagnosis in 1990 revealed his awareness then). He had lived his life the way he always had: with passion, determination, and a singular focus. Obviously, this was about to change. Now, his reality was shaken. He was vulnerable and scared. This news and his unusual display of emotion had broken him *open*; now he had nowhere to turn but inward. My clarity was unwavering. I knew I was ready (feeling quietly called) to walk beside him no matter what might transpire.

One evening, I read an article about death in the *Utne Reader* (Sept/Oct 1991). I was riveted by the opening sentence. It read: "Facing death—it's inevitable, it's difficult, and it might transform your life." Could this really be true? The idea that death could be transforming was, in itself, transforming to me. I had never thought of it in that way before. Pondering this idea further, I realized a new paradigm had presented itself. A seed was planted, giving me the opportunity to think about death in an entirely different way. I shared this with Dad as soon as I could. We both were transfixed by the idea. It resonated for us, for we knew there had to be more than just waiting for the body to die. From that moment forward, we joined. We entered into a new understanding that his diagnosis along with his pending death could be an invitation to healing for us both. Neither one of us hesitated. We immediately opened to the possibility of transformation, despite not having any idea how that might occur.

We lived with measured time, doing our best to make the most of it. One day, Dad called, saying, "Honey, do you think you could get away from work so the two of us could go on a picnic?" This was an idea I think Corrine helped foster, but Dad initiated. It was definitely novel! I was further touched when he said he would make our lunches if I would do the driving. Wow! Such a departure from the past. I was overjoyed.

It was easier to get together now that he and Corrine had moved even closer to us. I took a day off from work to avoid weekend traffic as we made our plan. He was elated. Dad made sure I knew he would include our favorite foods, especially that he would not forget the drinks. My heart burst with love at hearing his plans. This was a part of him I had longed to see. But up until this moment, the unwanted legacies from so many past wounds had dictated otherwise. Now, his heart was wide open, showing him to be thoughtful and committed to being together.

Our first picnic together turned out to be quite special. It paved the way for more. At any given time, I could either be moved to tears knowing I was saying goodbye to him or I could be laughing at his hilarious jokes. He could be really funny. There was no pretense. No masks. No roles. Just our true selves together.

A vintage photo taken of me and Dad on one of our picnic days in Julian, CA, a year before he died.

Every few weeks I made sure to take time away from work. Together we chose the right day and the right place for our next picnic, Dad as lunch-maker and me as driver. Our conversations were open. No topic was off limits. At last he wanted to know about me and my life. We stayed true to our commitment—just us, one-on-one. He reflected on his years of drinking; I reflected on my years of anger mixed with disappointment and resentment. I also noted his courage to enter recovery. He reflected on my steadfastness to stay the course before and after he did. He noted his regret at not being the best husband to Mom or the best father to me. I acknowledged his blind spots, noting how his early childhood had surely shaped him to be as he was, as we all are...flawed and human. Each picnic allowed our hearts to expand. We were healing at a level beyond the barricade of past wounds.

I was even able to tell him how deeply hurt I had been when he had not been available to celebrate my last birthday. Yes, we had gotten together later, but I had not been able to speak of my festering deep-felt rejection until now. When I finished sharing, he quietly shook his head as though seeing for the first time the effect his self-centeredness had on those he loved most. He apologized, acknowledging how deeply affected I had been. Sharing something I have never forgotten, he said with tears in his eyes, "Honey, I have always appreciated how well you've known me. You have always been willing to share your heart with me." Tears flowed down my cheeks as I realized how long I had waited to hear those very words. Yes, I had shared my heart with him on numerous occasions, only to feel shattered by his rejection. Although now, I knew, without reservation, that his apology was truly heartfelt. Finally, this wound could begin to heal.

Countless times, our hearts had opened to one another, only to close from the thorns within our relationship. We had arrived at a new place where this threat loomed once more, but somehow, I felt this moment promised to be a greater opening than any before. I felt so deeply grateful for this precious gift. It was a treasured opportunity for deeper connection.

We always knew we had only *this moment in time.* No other. The next moment would present itself soon enough. The only thing we knew for sure was each moment would require us to stay open to face it with courage as best we could...together.

Chapter 11

The Presence of Grace

E ven though my dad and I were ready for a new, more empowering perspective around the idea of death, we still had old beliefs that challenged us. The biggest one dictated death would be our final separation once his body died. Neither one of us were sure if life in some form would continue; privately, we hoped it would. I quietly wondered if any of our unfinished issues might remain just that, unfinished. I also wondered if I could embrace his passing remembering our fond memories and joy or I would be seduced into feeling endlessly sad, believing a life worth living meant you carried some degree of suffering, like a badge of honor. Despite this cultural script, we never hesitated to commit to being open to explore any questions that centered around death or unfinished issues between us. It seemed like a force that locked our focus on one thing, and one thing only: being open to the truth of anything standing in our way as father and daughter. Together, we reaffirmed our decision to be open on all matters, difficult or not, not fully realizing how challenging that would be.

One evening, as we sat together in his den, he brought up the subject of money. With regret in his voice, he admitted, "Honey, I'm sorry I won't be leaving you with much money after I die."

I was shocked. I had no idea this had been a disappointment for him until now. We had agreed to discuss any prevailing concerns. Surprisingly, this was one of his. Looking him straight in the eye, I said: "Dad, this hardly matters to me. What we now have is priceless," referring to our long struggle toward union and partnership.

His smile conveyed his deep appreciation of what it had taken to get to this point. But he pressed on. His voice was tentative as he asked, "Do you remember the money Mom left you in her savings account after she died?"

"Yes, of course," I said. I added, "You weren't happy about the fact she had never told you about it. Besides your name wasn't even on the account."

"Yes, that's right. I was surprised she did that, not telling me anything about it."

"No kidding!" I said to myself, inwardly rolling my eyes. That was a definite *understatement*, for I suspected they had had secrets around money. Not with big things, like the purchase of a car or a new home. They usually agreed there. Both harbored insecurities, nonetheless. Mom had been used to earning her own money long before she met Dad. When she went back to work part-time, once I had moved out, she told me had Dad wanted to not only see her monthly paycheck, but deposit it himself. What's with that? He could be controlling, definitely chauvinistic given the era he was raised in.

He wanted all monies to be in their joint account where he could keep his eye on them. Being raised during the Great Depression, Dad knew what it was like to live without enough money; scarcity was very real to him. Mom had not always been open or honest around money, either. Many women were not at the time. They relied on men for their financial welfare, often resorting to hiding what money they could in case of an emergency…it was one way to feel secure.

I knew my dad had been pissed upon discovery of Mom's bank passbook in her dresser drawer after she had died. I could see the irritation on his face as he tried to restrain his emotion that day. Here was something he did not know anything about. Discovering this secret, he probably wondered what else had he not known about. He had asked me about this at the time. As I told him what had transpired, I realized for the first time she had never discussed it with him. Mom had told me she wanted "some money of her own" in case something happened to Dad (which I had translated to mean she was worried she would not have immediate access to money in case he killed himself or others in a five-car pile-up on the freeway due to his out-of-control drinking). I shared these recollections then added: "Dad, your drinking was so out of control at that time. Mom was terrified that something catastrophic would happen, leaving her without immediate funds." Even with this explanation at the time, he could not get past it. He stewed about it for days.

Month after month went by, the secret savings account never being addressed. One night, however, while on the phone, he brought it up. He asked me if I had any plans for the money. I did not. Being so busy with graduate school and family, I had not thought any further about it. I had transferred the money to a savings account at my local bank for the time being.

"What would you think about investing the money together? I will match what she left you. Together we can find an investment fund that will bring a solid return. I have several in mind." (Dad had always been a successful self-taught investor.) I saw no reason to say no at the time. Part of me even looked forward to sharing in a project together.

Returning to our current conversation and his question, I said, "Yes, of course I remember when we invested our monies together," feeling happy about our decision to work in this manner. "How is the fund doing, by the way?"

Not answering my last question, he looked down, avoiding my gaze, then blurted out, "Well, we don't have that investment anymore."

Stunned, I had to catch my breath before I could question him further. Sighing deeply, I said with undisguised irritation in my voice, "What do you mean we don't have our investment anymore?"

Suddenly, it was a *very awkward* moment between us. I could tell he did not want to answer my question. But I persisted.

Slowly, he admitted what he had done: "I cashed it out."

"What…you cashed it out? Why in the world would you do that?" I gasped, as I started to feel a blanket of dread surround me; I knew this conversation was not headed anywhere good. For the life of me, I could not figure out why he would do such a thing without talking to me first. Not giving in to his reluctance to say anything further, I pressed him for the answer.

As embarrassment flickered in his eyes followed by shame in his voice, he painfully said, "I was worried… I didn't think I would have enough money to pay for my medical expenses."

As his words sunk in, I felt so disheartened. When were the betrayals ever going to stop? Then a surge of anger kicked in. Mom had been deceptive about money with Dad. Now he had been deceptive with me. I felt the sting from another betrayal. "He can be such a jerk," I muttered to myself. "I just want to shake him until he snaps out of this stupid behavior, then talk some sense into him!" Each spark of anger ignited another round of outrage from past hurts that whirled around in my mind. I listened to the litany of old wounds give voice to another insult that I wanted to hurl back at him. I resisted saying anything. I stayed silent for a long moment, in my uncertainty about what was next. Taking deep breaths, I tried to let my feelings settle. As I did, I suddenly was met with another stunning revelation: Dad had never put my name on the investment account. Only his. If he had, he would have needed my permission to liquidate the funds. Wow, had I ever been naïve! I had trusted he would have my best interests in mind…and he did not. In a flash, I felt set up plus taken advantage of. Furthermore, I felt stupid being blindsided like this. I had years of practice trying to protect myself at all costs as Dad's drinking created constant chaos in my life. I had learned vigilance, always scanning my surroundings for potential fallout. Now that my dad had been in recovery for over nine years, I had thought it was no longer required. I had certainly been mistaken.

Putting that aside for the moment, I knew he had good medical coverage, along with a decent savings account, for I had taken over paying his bills and reconciling his bank statement at his request. He could trust me with his daily finances, so why not a joint investment? If he had told me of his worry, of course, I would have agreed to liquidate the fund. Even at this point in his life, though, here he was still so conditioned not to rely on or trust anyone with specific issues, not even me, as his daughter. Now, it involved money. All this time I had mistakenly thought we still had our investment together. Instead we were facing another threat to our newly forged partnership, now tenuously hanging by a thin thread.

As I drove home that night I vented my outrage, relieved no one was around to hear it. "Holy crap, how could he do such a thing?" If it was not one thing, it was another, giving our relationship an UP and DOWN quality that had worn me out. I heard a litany of doubts voice themselves, each speaking of their pain. Why was I a disappointment to him? Why would he not let me be his confidante? Why would he not trust me? Once I heard my pain out loud, I slowly realized something new: these questions were not about my failings. Instead, they signaled my doubts about him...was he a disappointment to me? Would I let him be my confidante? Would I let myself rely on him? Able to finally focus on myself, the raw truth had emerged: I did not believe I could trust him.

For days, I was spun around by this deception. It was so very difficult to grasp he would do such a thing, *to me*. Had I been naive to think our trust was solid? What was I to do with this news? Overlook it? Be angry about it? Have this permanently rupture our relationship altogether? In the words of Raven, one of my Native American teachers, as one prepared for death, it was a time to finish what we could with clear eyes and clean hands. Nevertheless, I could not help but wonder if or when the blows to our relationship would *ever end*. Yes, we had agreed to be open with one another. I just had had no idea how hard it would be to honor that promise. The cancer was advancing ever since his bone marrow biopsy nine months before indicated it had metastasized to the bone, making it clear that Dad was not well-equipped to resolve this matter with me. As he was nearing the time of increased doses of morphine for his pain, I was resigned. And heartsick. Sadly, what was done, was done. Clearly, this issue would find an outlet only between me and my therapist.

By January 1994, Dad stopped looking for other options for his healing. Knowing that conventional medicine had nothing further to offer (told to us earlier by the don't-buy-any green-bananas oncologist), we had investigated how natural medicine might help. In the end, even though there were possibilities, he decided to forgo them. He said he just wanted to live his life the way he always had, eating what he liked; no wheat grass, juicing, or tofu for him. It had been almost four years since his initial diagnosis of prostate cancer. Now my heart felt heavy hearing his decision. Yet, both Corrine and I accepted it the best we could. We had known this day would come at some point. Now, it was here.

All along, our commitment had been to be open about everything. Now, I realized we had an adapted version of that promise. We would be forthcoming as much as was *humanly* possible. I knew Dad was flawed. Besides, I was coming to the conclusion that I was, too. Our circumstances precluded perfect closure. It was messy... and so uncomfortable. Wrestling this reality had heightened my frustrations, day after day. I wanted to change our relationship into a Hallmark version, instead of what we had. I sat in Jan's office one day recounting these very frustrations to him. I reiterated the many ways I wanted perfect closure with my dad. How I wished he were different next to the many ways we were different. Jan's silence told me there was something deeper beginning to surface within me. I waited. I listened more deeply. Finally, I heard what I needed to know: acceptance and forgiveness now needed to lead the way. Was I up to this task? Could I really forgive him? Could I accept all that had torn us apart...even things I might not know anything about until later? Countless times I thought I had done just that, accepted the ugliness and disappointment he brought to our relationship. But now, I had come to the place where acceptance was the only way. What was being asked of me was an order of magnitude greater than anything I had ever faced.

Somewhere deep within, I knew I had to try. It was just my nature. Even though I still felt the sting of some of the things he had chosen to reveal (which I had brought to therapy), I followed this new voice within, a wise voice which kept me focused on letting go, letting love and forgiveness lead the way. There was no roadmap telling me how to do this. I just knew I had to trust how this new path would unfold. It was untrodden, making me feel vulnerable and inept.

I re-entered our commitment with new eyes and ears. I kept my heart open, staying in the present as much as possible. As Dad's health steadily declined, I mustered up the courage to ask him an obvious question: "Dad, how do you want to die?"

With clarity he said simply: "I want to die at home with the help of hospice."

At this moment, I loved his courage to say what he wanted in spite of ALL the challenges we had confronted. He had obviously been thinking about this very question. In this bittersweet moment, I was able to feel grateful for what honesty he could display. This clearly showed us our next step.

By early March, we had investigated various hospice programs along with interviewing their personnel. It was a good thing, for within two weeks we were in need of their services. Our first crisis happened while Ken and I were having lunch at Dad and Corrine's home one day. When my dad tried to get up from the kitchen table, his body suddenly froze mid-way. He could not sit back down or stand fully erect, nor could he speak. He was stuck, unable to move or talk. Ken immediately steadied him. Together they waited for Dad to stand on his own. But he could not. His body refused to move, leaving all of us stunned and unnerved.

Instantly, I felt a loving and benevolent energy enter in, while my tall and strong husband embraced Dad's 5'10" frame, lifting his now lighter 140-pound body, carrying him down the hallway to the bedroom. As he gently put him down to rest, I watched from the kitchen knowing that something shocking yet beautiful had just happened. Even though it was a clear sign that Dad's body was wearing out, I watched my two favorite men together in a most vulnerable way, absent of ego or pretense, young taking care of old, a son-in-law stepping up to do what his father-in-law could no longer do, with respect, dignity and love.

Grace-like energy had certainly shown up that day. It found us where we were, but did not leave us where we had been. I felt held by it, much like I had after Mom had died. I had had other moments when this grace-like energy swept over me in the past. Though I always felt there was something mysterious about it, its arrival was undeniable, ushering in with it an uncompromising presence of loving-kindness and peace. Here it was once again.

By mid-March, hospice was ever-present. With efficiency, exceptional kindness and goodness, they provided all that my dad needed as well as what Corrine and I wanted. They answered my many questions: How does a body die? What should I be alert to? What should I do in case of emergency? How do I be present with the dying process? Their heart-soothing answer to this last question was: Just be in this moment. Let love surround you both. No need to resist or insist. We could not have asked for anything more. I took care of Dad most weekend nights so Corrine could rest. It was the one time I could be with him while I worked during the week.

Even though our last conversation had brought a painful betrayal to light, miraculously, as I stayed open to love, regardless of the past, our bond of love returned again and again. I had stepped away from my anger, putting my mistrust of him aside. My wounds were healing in other ways. Love was helping us find our way to continue our open-hearted talks. One night, as he reflected on his career, he shared how he had been so happy to have been able to collaborate over the years with his brother, Herb, about how to increase and diversify his crop production, plus how to streamline management on his farm land in Weston. Within a short time, Dad's guidance, culled from his schooling and years of professional experience, brought about the success for his brother they had both hoped for.

He also spoke about his three siblings. Even though they had married and had children of their own, communication remained limited. This was partly due to living in different states and partly due to economics. It was not easy to stay in touch other than by an occasional long-distance phone call (which was very expensive at the time) or a yearly Christmas card. Visits happened, but were rare. However, once all of their children became independent in their own lives, the siblings had decided to have a reunion at their oldest sister's home in Washington State. This reunion had also included their mother, Alta. For the first time since early childhood, he and his siblings were all together. Despite the fact Dad was still drinking (sobriety would come one year later), he said it had been a very special weekend for him, one he never forgot.

At a second reunion that followed five years later, those who could joined in what turned out to be their final gathering. Knowing he was sober at that time, I prompted him to compare the two experiences.

"Herb was still actively drinking and smoking. I had visited with him earlier and shared about my newfound sobriety, telling him how at peace I felt for the first time in my life. I asked him if he was interested in no longer drinking? Sadly, he said he saw no point in it. He was happy the way he was."

"Dad, what was that like for you to hear, your dear brother clearly choosing addiction?"

"I wished he had been open to the choice, but it was out of my hands."

In spite of Herb's decision, he still was deeply grateful they had created the opportunity to reconnect, for two years later, Dad's youngest sister, Lila, died, followed by his oldest sister Muriel two years later, then finally Herb—all within a four-year period. My dad was the sole survivor, outliving his brother by six years. Despite their difficult early circumstances, love had endured through many difficult times—in spite of addiction—and found its way back.

Dad's condition seemed to plateau for a while. Hospice care brought stability and peace to our lives. Gratitude co-existed next to uncertainty over what the next moment would bring. Day by day, I tried my best to stay present. One day while at work I got a call from Corrine. "Your dad has taken a turn for the worse. They're not sure what has happened, but you will probably want to come as soon as you can." I was shaken by the news, but not surprised. I alerted Ken while leaving work in the middle of the day. My mind raced as I traveled the familiar 65 miles from work to their home. Very familiar questions were on my mind: will *this* be his last day? If so, what do I need to do to prepare myself? When no definitive answers came, I simply heeded the now-familiar advice: *Stay present. Stay open.* Once I arrived, we had a tense few hours, but he stabilized. I stayed a bit longer in case there was anything further I could do. When there was not, I said goodbye to Corrine then got in the car to drive home. This drive had become *very* familiar; now I was making it weekly. Nothing told me this night would be any different from any other, yet I was in for a surprise.

Once on the highway, I started to process Dad's medical crisis. Taking some long deep breaths, I felt a profound sense of exhaustion, now coupled with my busy mind searching for what more I could do to take care of him. When my thoughts finally quieted, I realized Dad was in good hands. It was obviously me who was in need of care. I was clearly feeling the combined effects of what work required of me, the significant commute, and being with Dad in the final stage of his life, never knowing from day to day if this would be his last. I felt overwhelmed by it all. No answers came because there were none.

Suddenly, my interior car light came on. My over-functioning mind initially became irritated, noting this was another thing on my never-ending list of things I had no control over. I no sooner had this thought when the light suddenly went off...and the radio turned on...without my assistance. Things were becoming weirder, and I was exasperated. I had not turned on the radio for a reason . . . silence for the drive was what I had craved. As I reached to turn it off, music from a Christian radio station filled the car. The moment was surreal, since I know I did not have this station programmed into my list of usual choices.

Just as I had experienced before, I felt a sense of peace surround me. As the music filled the car, my worries instantly vanished. I felt held by a remarkable spiritual presence that lifted my fears, eliminated my doubts and filled me with a profound sense of love. Once I surrendered to the experience, the radio turned itself off as quickly as it had turned itself on. I did not know what to make of this. The more I tried to analyze it, the more my mind went quiet. I was held in this loving energy, limiting access to any of my usual faculties. It felt amazing.

When I returned home that night, I did not tell Ken about the experience, needing not only more rest, but time for the experience to settle in. When I woke the next morning, the feeling I had from the night before remained. I felt lighter, with an incredible sense of knowing all would be OK. When this peace remained for several more days, I decided to tell Ken what happened that night on my way home. In his quiet way he looked at me, never doubting my experience, saying he, too, was amazed, but not surprised, this had happened to me. I was not sure what to make of his response. He was usually more skeptical than I was about other-worldly matters. . . just not this time.

I felt anchored as never before. As a result, each change in Dad's condition failed to upend me for long. One day as I was taking care of him he said he wanted to plan his memorial service. "Of course, let's do that," I said, happy to have a focus. As Corrine and I sat next to him in his hospital bed, we made notes of what he wanted. Once we were done, I laughed out loud, for it struck me funny as to how would I communicate what we had just done to anyone outside of the conversation? How would I tell others that we consciously planned my dad's memorial service with him still being very much alive and in charge? It felt like we had broken a fundamental rule, by planning a loved one's service while that person was still living; surely it would be more respectful if we waited until after he died. There was that old belief again around pending death to only be whispered about or denied until the end.

For most of April, Dad was fairly ambulatory and able to participate in conversations. When he asked if we could celebrate Easter together at their home, we immediately agreed. Once we arrived, we noticed right away Corrine was distracted. She said she was upset that a close neighbor had just passed away a few hours before. All she could think was that from now on his family would no longer appreciate or even be able to celebrate Easter for the rest of their lives. Death made that determination in her mind. Really? For I had quite a different response, seeing Easter as a celebration of rebirth. With my newly adopted idea about death, I began to see it as a birth, only this time birthing into spirit.

Later, I asked Dad what he thought of his neighbor dying on Easter. He, too, did not see it as tragic. "I now believe there is continuity of life after death," he said. "I'm not quite sure where we have come from or where we might go once dead. But I clearly feel it's entirely possible we have been here before in other lifetimes. I don't believe death is the end; it's just the end of this phase before we go on to the next." Despite his compromised state, I was surprised by his clarity. He shared his philosophy as though it were second nature. I agreed, adding what I had come to realize. "You know, the many challenges and joys we have had as father and daughter, and as a family, have to be part of something larger. I don't believe what we have endured will be erased once you die. It has to be part of a larger plan...part of a larger purpose." I did not know how I knew that. I just did. It seemed to be part of a deeper knowing that kept emerging the more we talked about death.

In the weeks to come, our healing progressed: me healing into my life next to him healing into his pending death. I set the tone by mentally surrounding us both in love and light, choosing to be open to the moment. I set a favorite hawk feather next to a piece of turquoise on his bedside table. We both saw the hawk as the messenger from spirit, helping us see from a higher perspective anything blocking our freedom from flight. Raven had given me the turquoise stone to give to Dad, saying it would strengthen our bond of friendship, providing courage to assist him in his transition. Dad had his journey before him, and I had mine. Only my trusted therapist, close friends and family could support me at this time. I found great solace in reading various meditations which focused on the healing of mind and body. I was in need of both. My body had taken on a lot of responsibility in caring for him. My mind, at any given time, could temporarily be flooded by anxiety in anticipation of his imminent death.

As usual, I was prone to over-functioning, looking at every worst-case scenario about loss: being alone. Being sad forever. Believing death would end my connection to my dad. With my newfound perspective, I knew this was no longer true, although the closer his death appeared, the more my primitive brain saddled me with these old beliefs from the past.

To help me through this, I started each day by reading a meditation that focused on loving-kindness. I chose which additional meditation to fit where my body and mind were. Sometimes it might be about forgiveness. Other times, it was looking at how love was the bridge to the heart. Each meditation allowed me to enter into the moment regardless of what else was happening. For that, I was grateful.

One May night, I immersed myself once again in reading these meditations at Dad's bedside. When I finished, I began to observe him resting in the hospital bed in the living room; it was clear his body was nearing the end. He was being administered higher doses of morphine for the pain. I watched how he moved in and out of consciousness. As he appeared to be asleep, I turned to read another meditation, this one about letting go. It was just what I needed in that moment. I read it quietly to myself, appreciating every instruction. My breathing became slow and steady. I looked over at my dad, noting his breathing had done the same thing. Once again, I slowly breathed in then slowly breathed out. So did he. I realized we were synchronizing our breaths. It seems strange to say, but I felt more connected with him by breathing together. We were attuned in a way I had not experienced before.

I kept reading about the subject of letting go. Once done, I sat for a long moment reflecting on its meaning. Suddenly, Dad sat up then, speaking in a clear voice said, "Honey, I like that meditation, too. The one about letting go." Whoa, I thought to myself. This cannot be happening! I went over to him, sitting on the edge of the bed then read a few lines out loud. "Yes, that's the one." No sooner had that happened than we were instantly surrounded by an incredible loving energy. A powerful message followed: *"Death won't part you. Your relationship will continue, just in a different form."* My eyes became teary. Dad was clearly moved as well. We looked at each other for a long moment, intuitively knowing we had been spoken to by Spirit while being held by this extraordinary spiritual intelligence of Grace.

Any cognitive understanding of this amazing moment vanished. I knew something very profound had happened. Could I trust this experience? Or was I too exhausted to know what was real anymore? This could be wishful thinking on my part, knowing that I did not want to say goodbye to him for the last time. Not knowing what to do next, I suspended my doubt for the time being, staying focused on Dad's care. But, one thing was clear… I could not deny that something **BIG** and life-altering had just happened.

Two weeks later, he took his last breath. Until a few hours before he passed, I had been next to him in a new way. I chose to suspend all doubt about Spirit's message. I began to trust we could communicate telepathically. Many of the days and nights I was with him, I silently read meditations as a way to prepare us both for his departure. I had become a type of midwife for this transition. We had said all we needed to say. We had no regrets. All that remained was our sorely-tested and ever-lasting love. Feeling complete in this way allowed me to return home to have dinner with Ken, knowing Dad could pass at any time. Two hours after I was home, Corrine called to say he was gone.

~ↄ

My dad had started life in a small homestead cabin on the prairies of southern Idaho, faced many challenges in his alcoholic family, survived the Great Depression, been one of the first of his generation from his small town to graduate from college, found love, defended his country, had a family, achieved his greatest dreams, chose sobriety, and made amends. He left this life with clear eyes and clean hands. Despite all of the emotional pain I had incurred, I still treasured him. He had lived his life with courage and determination. He had been far from perfect, but he eventually stayed true to himself. He had admitted many of his failings, allowing himself to be vulnerable. Besides, he had opened his heart to me as best he could. This was his final gift… and it was a gift beyond measure.

Chapter 12

Navigating New Territory

I closed my eyes, while Ken drove me to Dad and Corrine's home, wondering what it would be like to see my dad, now dead. Suddenly, it dawned on me that I had never seen a dead person before. What would my dad look like? Would he look the way TV crime labs showed a dead body in a morgue? Pale and plastic-looking? Would I be frightened or repulsed? Or, would I….? I suddenly interrupted my imaginings, feeling irritated with myself. I needed to recognize the truth staring me in the face at this very moment. I did not like the unknown or the vulnerability that came with it. I was feeling both in a big way. No amount of wondering was going to help me forge a clear plan. I simply did not know what to expect. That was my Achilles heel. Years of focus on alcoholism in my family taught me to always have a plan. Now, the situation dictated I could not.

I took a deep breath once we entered the front door. I tried to be present, but felt pulled in several directions. The initial pull was to join Corrine, to see how she was coping. Next, I was pulled to follow Ken's lead. Then again, another part of me wanted to ignore both of those distractions, go straight to my dad's bedside to see for myself. Once I did, I suddenly felt suspended from my feelings, oddly detached. I felt like an observer as I saw him still lying in the hospital bed as though nothing had happened. Coming closer, I noticed that his skin was very pale, cool to the touch. His body looked like an empty shell. Like a scientist observing something new for the very first time, I whispered to myself, "Oh, this is what a body looks like when the life force is gone. What an extraordinary thing to witness." I glanced down at the carpet for a moment, taking in what I saw. My eyes softened. Suddenly, I felt pulled to look up and around the living room where Dad had spent the last two months of his life. When I did, I saw the entire living room filled with an iridescent light emitting a beautiful energy like nothing I had seen before. It was breathtaking. Instantly, my analytical mind was silenced. Intuitively, I just knew to take in this Light, letting it surround me. A few weeks earlier, Dad and I had experienced Light similar to this as Spirit told us we would be ever-connected. Now, here it was again in a new way. No question, I knew this was my dad's spirit. His essence was everywhere I looked. It took over the room, making his physical body seem quite insignificant. I did not think others noticed this in the way I did until Corrine came into the living room. Frequently plagued by anxiety in the months leading up to Dad's death, she surprisingly noted: "It feels so peaceful being in this room with your dad, like never before."

This extraordinary moment filled me with a feeling I can only describe as *love* in its purest form. It was to be the first of many experiences I would later have with my dad, when I would feel love in this new expanded way.

As I returned my attention back to Dad's body, I was acutely aware he was now free, released from the bondage of his disease. I felt relieved, not only for me, but for everyone involved. Strangely, guilt never entered in. I realized it did not need to. We had all done what we could to ensure ease and comfort from pain, and we had done it with love.

In short order, the plans Dad had so meticulously dictated for his memorial were put in place. Four days later, many who knew him came together to celebrate his life. Ken was my rock as he helped carry out our plans. Also offering me unlimited support were Dottie, as well as my forever-friend, Carolyn, who had traveled from Oregon to be by my side. My oldest stepson and his girlfriend also took time away from their college studies and work, to travel from Colorado to be a part of this experience. My heart burst with appreciation at the lengths people took to be present.

Dad had chosen the church and the minister for his service. He wanted others to be part of it, as well. Ken spoke about Dad's avid love of reading. He especially enjoyed poems and stories written by Rudyard Kipling. Ken read a selection entitled, "If," a poem written Kipling wrote in 1895. In it Kipling talks to his own son, giving him advice about the qualities important for manhood. He emphasizes the quality of leadership as being essential, most notably the necessity of trusting yourself no matter how destabilizing things might be around you. Knowing I would be too emotional to read my message,

I asked the minister to read in my place. I wrote about our joys and triumphs as well as our challenges. Adversity had certainly been an important teacher, without which we might not have experienced love in the way we did. One by one, others offered their touching remembrances to the point my heart simply could not take in anymore. I was overwhelmed by the love that surrounded me. At the same time, I was exhausted by the intensity of it all. While at the reception, as I regained some energy, I managed to take a long deep breath, looking around the room at the many people there. I did not want to miss an opportunity to simply take in what was happening. I saw the love that brought all of us together... love that could have only happened because of my dad.

The glow from Dad's memorial service lifted Corrine and I through the business we needed to tend to in the subsequent weeks. We were in touch daily, sometimes more often. One evening, after spending part of the day together at the attorney's office, she called to say she had felt sad once she returned home. The reality of Dad being gone had set in once again. As she made plans to eat dinner alone, suddenly everything changed, she said. "Your dad was here," she exclaimed. "Whenever I'm sad, he keeps turning on the stereo and playing our favorite song!" I laughed. Somehow this did not surprise me. I innately knew that was his way to be with Corrine in her lowest moments. Whenever she felt overwhelmingly sad about missing him, the stereo always came on, playing their favorite song. Regardless of whether it made rational sense or not, she said she could not remain sad for long, for she felt his love surround her. I knew, on some level, he was helping her know death was not the end of their love, only a transformation of it.

I felt Dad's love around me, too. Sometimes it came as a whisper, other times it came as a memory of something we had both found hilariously funny. At the same time, though, grief remained nearby. My mind could be repeatedly hijacked. It usually happened when I left the house to run errands. Once on the road, I found I could not remember where I was going or what I planned to do. Bless Ken, for it was more than I would like to admit that I called him asking him to remind me about what I was supposed to do. Even with a reminder, and the errands eventually completed, I felt like I was in a time warp.

I had not expected grief to show up in this way. In fact, in my naïveté, I had not expected it to show up at all. I had thought it would be easier because Dad and I had healed in so many ways. I truly felt his death was a birth for both of us. I had thought I was ready to move forward. But I soon realized there would be no forward movement for the time being. It became abundantly clear I was not in charge of much, if anything. Grief was in charge. It had a different plan and timeline altogether.

I rapidly learned grief meant not being able to read more than two sentences at a time; it meant I could walk into a room with intentions that suddenly vanished. I learned grief sheared away the mask of normal life, forcing brutal honesty out of my mouth before propriety could stop me. I had very few filters in place for a while, blurting out harsh words and feeling no remorse. Not long after Dad died, I was waiting in the checkout line at a local grocery store. I felt raw from my loss. Hearing people talk about so many meaningless things while in line triggered me. I brutally judged how stupid everyone's conversation was, shaking my head in disbelief. I had just said goodbye to my dad and I wanted every stranger around me to know it. How could they not know the loss of a loved one was far more important than discussing the latest tabloid headlines? I wished our culture had a tradition which could indicate to others you had experienced loss, like wearing black for a year used to signify; somehow my loss would not feel so invisible. I remembered feeling this same way nine years before when Mom had passed. I also remembered the urgency with which some people expressed their desire (or need) for me to move on. I wanted to move on, too. But, then as now, grief had a plan for me. Until I learned what was necessary, there would be no moving on. I also realized no two deaths represent the same level of loss or usher in the same grieving process. Reading a favorite book, *Companion Through the Darkness,* one night before bed, I was struck by this one succinct sentence: "Grief humbles. It shrouds. But eventually, it enlightens." So true. Clearly, I was light-years away from enlightenment; I hardly knew the concept, let alone how it would happen. I was in unchartered territory, clueless about my next step.

I was also in uncharted territory in other areas of my life. As I had entered into what would be the last year of my dad's life, I had made a decision to leave USD at the end of the academic year. It had not been an easy decision, but it was a necessary one. I was ready to establish a private practice and lessen my commute. Two months after Dad's death, I started a new chapter in my professional life. In my personal life, six weeks after my dad died Ken and I said goodbye to a favorite aunt. Then our precious dog, Chris, was diagnosed with cancer. How ironic for cancer to be central to my life, once again. I really had had my fill of draining emotions due to my dad's journey.

Now, I would be taking a similar journey with Chris. Once again, my "plate" was overflowing with a volume of loss I did not want to fully acknowledge. I just wanted to move on. The more I tried, the more I felt I was in quicksand. The more I tried to think my way through my grief, the more frustrated I became. Once again, I was reminded that less was more; the less I tried to think, the more I was able to listen to my heart. That meant I had to be still, sitting in the unknown, and in the place of "I don't know." I hated the idea; my intuition told me it was the only way through. I had to trust what I did not "know." There simply was no other way. By its very nature, grief held me in its grip, insisting I surrender to its power.

With ongoing support from my therapist, Jan, I gradually opened to exploring all that was coming up for me. He had guided me through the last four years of Dad's transition, and numerous work-related issues, as well as relationship challenges. Now he was the right person to help me navigate this new territory, as well. My emotional flood gates opened, overwhelming me by their startling revelations. There was no shortage of things I needed to process. We no more than finished one thing when the next thing rushed in to fill its place.

Anniversaries often trigger grief. Dad's birthday, three months later, left me raw. In August, I celebrated his birthday for the first time without him. Corrine and I went to the Riverside National Cemetery across from March Air Force Base where his ashes were buried. Afterward, during lunch we talked about the ways in which we missed him. I appreciated her openness. I felt her love for him. But later, alone and journaling about my own feelings, my outer resolve disappeared, leaving me to face what I had not been able to let myself face until now. I could not believe I would never touch him again, never feel the hands that had held me as a baby, reassured me as a child, and danced with me as an adult. Those hands had connected us throughout our 47 years together. Now they were gone. Such finality. It was stunning. I could not seem to get used to it. It left me irritated, often raw at times. I felt as though I had no skin to protect me. Part of me could not believe I felt this way...it was so irrational. Yet, my feelings ruled. They took me where they needed me to go. Each feeling told a story. In the early months after Dad's death, I relived his physical decline any time I saw an older person exhibiting similar limitations. The way they walked or the paleness of their aging skin froze me in my tracks. I felt my own limitations, my own powerlessness to do anything about it. Any time someone I knew was diagnosed with cancer, it was like a jolt back to the day my dad learned of his diagnosis. Only this time, I had more perspective...I knew the walk would be arduous.

I was being revisited by the old childhood pattern of feeling scared and lonely. Emotional abandonment was at the core. I could not believe how difficult it had been for my dad to be emotionally present with me as I was growing up or how responsible I felt for the disconnection. It had been an endless cycle of trying to fix what was broken between us, only to be met by more rejection.

A theme emerged in some of my early dreams after Dad's death that indicated how off-center and vulnerable I felt. In one dream, I walked down a road only to hear the thunderous roar of water rushing up behind me; before I could even turn around, I was immediately swept up in the current. I had this dream repeatedly until I became more resilient through Jan's support. He sat with me as I acknowledged my fears, explored each one, finding the truth hidden beneath the scary exterior. The more I did this, the more resilient I became. Eventually, the dream showed me standing off to the side as the rushing water created its own channel. I was beginning to find my emotional footing with feelings I never thought I had. I was no longer as frightened of the unknown. I still did not like it, but I knew I could find safety. As time went by, I grew to expect the unknown, to not be surprised by new issues arising that I had no previous awareness of. I learned to lean into each discovery. I learned to listen to and trust my intuition. I learned ways to keep myself from feeling overwhelmed.

Even though I kept listening to every feeling, there still was a big part of me that just wanted the grief to be gone, once and for all. Staying present to emotions was hard work. Sometimes, I felt like I was running a marathon for the first time. I just wanted to cross the finish line. I turned to several books to give me much-needed insight and comfort. I learned most people are tempted to put their grief behind them during the long middle phase of grieving (which was where I was); they want to return to a normal life, ignoring all that seeks to break down the world as they had known it. That was me. But, at the same time, I knew I would never be the same; I could never return to my life as it had been: It had been unalterably changed.

This was not an accidental discovery. It came from fighting my grief while struggling to resurrect the emotional structures which had crumbled. It was a struggle that only yielded desperation, which forced the understanding once again, that willpower had no place here. Something greater than I was at work. When I began to surrender to it, my perspectives could be altered by the minute. This phase lasted for what felt like months of relentless darkness while I felt completely adrift.

The theme of disorientation seemed to be everywhere. Up felt like down. Activities I had used to enjoy left me empty. The vegetable garden Ken had helped me plant while Dad helped me tend lay fallow. Even the bench Ken had built for my dad to sit on looked sadly empty. I could not bring myself to look at it. My world had gone from Technicolor® to black and white. No matter how much I wanted it to be otherwise, grief now felt a lot like depression. I had little energy. I was apathetic about most things. I had little to no interest in exercising. Food was an afterthought.

As I slowly began to fully accept most of what Dad's death represented for me, I was struck by another jolting revelation. I realized my grief was now twofold: I was grieving not just my loss of my dad, but also the loss of Mom. At first, I could not believe this was possible. I had grieved my mom's departure long ago. But no. Now, I had to face this undeniably harsh reality: I no longer had either of my parents in my everyday life. Mom's death represented one reality, Dad's death another. Now I was peeling back layers of grief represented by both of them being my parents.

I was learning that feelings have a very circuitous manner in which they surface. Somehow, they brought me head-on to face a core sense of shame I had carried for years. While I felt I had accepted the shame my parents had both felt about themselves, I also understood I had taken on some of it as my own. Knowing this, Jan introduced a way of healing this wound through guided imagery. In one session, with his guidance, I imagine I am with my dad as we sit at sunset on the sand in front of a small fire at a favorite beach in Oregon. I tell him how shame has affected my life—how it immobilizes me from accessing my inner resources. I am frightened and angry at myself when I hear an inner voice say, "Shame on you for being this way." Dad tells me of his newfound comprehension of the depth of his shame from spirit, sharing he had always felt inferior and inadequate. He had constantly fought against it by overachieving.

I invite Mom to join us. She tells of her shame being a woman, how inferior she felt at times. She added how angry she was at her father for constantly devaluing her. We gather wood from nearby that represents the size of our shame. Dad's piece is large, making it hard to manage. He puts it in the fire, but it is slow to burn. Together, we split it into smaller pieces, which finally enables the fire to take hold. Mom's piece is smaller. She puts it in the fire where, in time, it, too, is consumed by the flames. My piece is smaller still. However, it is dense and heavy. I put it in the flames, watching it dissolve to ash. As the flames effectively dissolve our shame, the three of us join hands. As we feel the shame vanish from our hearts, a white bird appears, joins us, surrounding us in white light. This ceremony instantly frees us from the burden we had carried for so long. As if by magic, in that one single session with Jan, this long-hidden layer of shame feels transmuted, abruptly void of any toxicity.

Jan's guidance helped me in utilizing the technique of guided imagery. It always brought me deep-lasting healing in ways I could rarely, if ever, define, even now as I write about it. The experiences felt authentic and very powerful. I wanted to share these amazing experiences with others, just as I want to share them here, but sadly, I fear much is lost in the translation.

Every step forward, however, always yielded a step back. Grief broadsided me in ways I never expected. The fact that my parents were no longer part of my everyday life consumed me. They had made my being here possible. Now they were gone. I just could not get my head wrapped around that. One night, as I sat in a hospice grief support group meeting that I attended regularly, I listened to what others had to share about their journeys with loss. When one seasoned member shared her past painful journey with grief, I asked her what helped her the most. She offered this: "When the pain of grief was at its greatest for me, I would imagine myself laying down beside a favorite river and letting God take care of me." For whatever reason, that seemed to be the perfect message for me. It resonated deeply. Then, whenever I reverted to my old ways of working, trying to overthink things, wanting to have order and control, and failing miserably, I began using the beautiful and soothing image of me lying by the river being held by Spirit. I was again learning about surrender.

As the first year drew to a close, I wondered how to be present with Dad on the anniversary of his passing. Jan had been teaching me how an anniversary could be a positive experience, one that could empower you instead of being overrun by sadness. Suddenly, I got the idea to plant California poppies all over our property. After all, Poppy was the name I had chosen for him years ago.

I chose a group of poppies to transplant on my property from several plants I found growing in the wild close to where I lived. With each one I planted, I felt my dad's presence, for he loved gardening. I felt happy to be together in a new way. I met Corrine for lunch. Together we once again visited the cemetery, being with him and other veterans whose service he so valued. Once I returned home,

I opened my desk drawer to find the watch Dad had been wearing before he died. For some reason, it had been one of the personal items I kept upon his passing. When he no longer wore it in the last few months of his life, he had kept it on a small side table by his hospital bed. After he had stopped wearing his glasses, he frequently asked me what time it was. It was such a part of him in the most everyday way. Seeing his watch in the drawer that evening brought back a rush of fond memories. In a flash, I saw him put on his watch after his morning shower as he got ready for the day. It was his timepiece, perpetually orienting him throughout each day, month and year. Taking it out of the drawer and holding it in my hands, I felt his energy. Once I looked at the face of the watch, I did a double take. I realized for the first time the hands had stopped at the exact moment of his death the year before. While his physical life here had ended then, the presence of poppies now brought visibility to his ongoing presence. Every spring and summer since, the poppies multiply on my property. It is a delightful surprise when I see them blooming because it brings Dad's love back to me.

After a year, the grieving process seemed to loosen its grip. I knew I was not done, for I was still faced with times when the sense of loss was almost unbearable. But overall, I just felt freer. Grief had been an amazing teacher. It would prove to be an ally as I prepared to take the next step on my journey with my dad.

THE RETURN TO SPIRIT'S PROMISE

Chapter 13

Whisperings

I remembered Spirit's promise before my dad had passed: that death would not part us as we opened to communicate telepathically. Rarely, however, had I given the idea further thought. Doing so pulled me out of my comfort zone, not knowing how to step into this possibility. What consumed me more were the changes grief thrust in my face. Added to the lessons I was trying to learn from grief was the daunting and exciting venture of establishing my private practice as a psychologist. Not ever having had a small business brought me a set of new challenges. That is where I chose to put my attention. In the midst of this transition, however, the quiet urge to discover what Spirit's promise might bring remained.

I saw Jan on a regular basis. He knew about Spirit's promise; I had told him one day when feeling especially brave, not expecting much of a response. Instead, his response had surprised me: sitting up in his chair, leaning into every word I said. The look on his face told me he took this promise seriously. Much more than I did, that is for sure. I knew if I explored this possibility further, it would pull me into unknown territory. *Very unknown.* Frankly, I had had enough new territory to deal with. Having been in a deeply uncomfortable zone for so long, I just wanted to retreat to something familiar, stay there and rest.

Sensing this, Jan invited me to begin exploring the feelings that held me back: doubt, distrust, and fear emerged in capital letters. A litany of questions followed: Did I imagine this promise? Was it even credible? How would I talk about this promise to Ken and my closest friends? Would it affect the way they saw me? Lastly, how would my colleagues view me if I told them I had an ongoing relationship with my dad, who was...dead? Frankly, at the end of the day, it all seemed too weird to me. However, despite my reticence, that part of me which kept asking for confirmation held firm. It wanted to forge ahead to discover the truth: would it be possible to communicate with my dad in a whole new way?

Each week in Jan's office, I came to understand the various meanings behind the doubts, the fears, and what threatened my credibility. I explored my fear of being discounted or rejected. I explored the possibility I might even lose friends. Some of my colleagues might distance themselves from me, not wanting to refer future clients to me. One of my deepest fears was that I might have imagined Spirit's promise. This possibility made me wonder if I could even trust its validity. Even if this promise were true, how would I know what to do? Would I do it right? (It was so much a part of my nature to think there was a prescribed way to do everything; I wanted a manual that would tell me step-by-step how to proceed.)

One by one, I addressed each fear. Eventually, I felt more grounded so that when Jan asked me, one day, if I wanted to contact my dad, I was finally ready. Being well-versed with Jan's level of expertise and competence, I agreed, knowing I would be fully supported in this experience.

At Jan's suggestion, I deepened my breathing, relaxed my body and mind to settle into a quiet meditative space. Jan set the intention for me to connect to Dad in a safe place. I immediately found myself in a beautiful forest of tall fir trees. Once there, I asked my dad to be present with me. In less time than it took for me to make the request, he was there, in my mind's eye, looking like he had in his 50s, casually dressed in work pants and a short-sleeved shirt. Like ESP, our thoughts were communicated to one another at lightning speed. It took little effort. Being together in this way felt amazing: so undeniably real, while at the same time, otherworldly. I felt surprisingly safe despite how new it was for me. As we stood facing each other in the clearing of this beautiful forest, the love that surrounded us was astounding—it was so pure and powerful. It became the "air we breathed" while together. I had never experienced anything so exquisitely touching. Next, he handed me a lovely bouquet of yellow roses and gardenias. *"Flowers are the language of love,"* he communicated in a flash even though his mouth never moved. His eyes emanated an extraordinary light, so full of love. It was as though the words came directly from his heart to mine. I was shocked he somehow remembered I appreciated flowers, along with their symbolism. As my dad, he rarely had any interest in symbolism, often dismissing the fact that I did. *"Roses can represent the transcendence of the human spirit, unity and spiritual love,"* he clarified. My head was spinning, finding it hard to process his new perspective, but I kept listening. I wondered how he knew any of this. I noted how the words he chose were so different from any words I would use…or words he would have used when he had been my dad. When he added that *"Yellow roses often symbolize friendship, joy and delight,"* I immediately understood the deeper meaning of this gift. He was speaking to me heart-to-heart, somehow knowing this was a language I would understand. *"Gardenias, suggesting the beginning of a budding love as well as healing,"* communicated what Poppy wanted for us: love and healing. My heart openly knew his intentions were true.

Just as I was about to ask him to expand on how we might be together in this way, he said: *"Dear one, stay with me, bring your love."* My heart leapt at the suggestion. I wanted to clarify what I needed from him before moving forward. *"Poppy,"* I said, *"Can you be open to ALL of my feelings? Are you willing to see me without any reservations?"* Showing all of me to my dad had always been risky in the past. I usually felt dismissed, discounted or misunderstood. The resulting wounds had always made me leery around him, especially when dealing with matters close to my heart. Lacking any hesitation, though, he passionately agreed, surrounding me in an amazing swirl of pink light. This interaction had not taken more than twenty minutes. Yet while the connection had been limited in real time, I felt we had traveled together in this manner for years.

Then my mind flashed back to his life here as I thought about some of the unresolved questions I still had. Feeling secure in our new relationship, I ventured forward, addressing two major questions. I first asked him why he had drunk. I followed this question by asking why he had been so depressed during several years of his life.

Without hesitation or ego, he replied, *"It was a bad time in my life. I felt sorry for myself, my loss of a dream."* I instantly knew he was referring to the loss of his beloved company. It represented a lifelong dream. In a flash, he showed me a replay of all he had done to make his passion possible. It was like watching a movie as I felt his elation at accomplishing what he had set out to do. The next scene showed darkness surrounding him during the height of his alcoholic years threatening to end his life, alongside all he cherished. He immediately verified what I felt. My heart opened to ALL of him in that instant: his vulnerabilities, his foibles, his addiction and insensitivities. I saw him only through the eyes of love. There was no room for any other perspective, only love.

As I quietly reveled in the love I felt for him, he went on to say, *"I haven't been there for you. I feel very bad about that. I was limited. I want that to change. Flowers are our way."* Poppy was truly ready to see me and hear me in ways I had always longed for. That, in itself, was unprecedented. For him to see the ways in which he had been limited was surprising. Absent from his demeanor was any ego or need to defend himself. He existed solely in the truth of it all.

I was so deeply moved by his gifts and admissions, copious tears streamed down my face as I felt the expansiveness of the love that now embraced us. To hear him speak this openly about some of his deepest struggles brought new light to the past. I began to link his past with what I had experienced as his daughter in an even deeper way. Even though he used few words most of the time, I intuitively knew the deeper meaning. Without a doubt, our hearts were wide open. We were eager to usher in the possibility of healing to a whole new level.

In spite of this extraordinary experience with my dad that day in Jan's office, and even with Jan encouraging me to invite this in on my own, I could still feel uneasy at a moment's notice. I felt I had to hide this very unconventional way of communicating despite the fact it brought me such joy. Other than sharing a few experiences with Ken, I told no one, keeping them between me and my journal.

Several times a year, I looked forward to consulting with my valued metaphysical teacher and advisor, Barbra Dillenger. I always appreciated advice from a metaphysical perspective. I found insights that complemented what I knew from a clinical point of view. She had studied psychology for years, but found her passion when she got her doctorate in divinity and metaphysics. She had a busy practice, and counted many professional people as clients. I appreciated her straightforward, supportive manner. There was nothing "woo-woo" about her. She was equally grounded both in reality and in spirit. This time was no different. As our session began, she started to share some of her general insights, but quickly stopped, interrupting her own train of thought. She stayed silent for a moment gathering her thoughts. With commanding clarity she said in a determined voice: "I'm getting the message that your dad wants to talk with you more!" Caught off guard for the moment, I sat speechless. I had not mentioned Spirit's promise or even about the few times I had talked to my dad after he passed. Or about my ambivalence about this way of connecting. As I shared about it, Barbra was unfazed by my ambivalence. She had clearly heard Poppy's wish; she was not going to ignore it. From that moment on, she proceeded to teach me more about conversing with my dad in spirit, which included how to prepare my journal, how to set my intention, as well as how to protect and ground myself for more of this type of communication. My head was reeling from everything she offered; I could hardly keep up. My heart, however, was engaged in every word she said.

Still, the feeling of being split in two remained. My head told me this was crazy, but my heart longed for more of this new level of connection. What was I going to do? It was obvious I had obstacles to confront—all within myself—before I would be fully comfortable with this new way of being in a relationship. My biggest struggle came from being a psychologist. I fretted, wondering what my colleagues would think if they knew I communicated in this way. Truthfully, I was talking to a dead person. Would they think I was crazy to be able to hear and see things from another dimension?

Eventually, I brought these concerns to both Jan and Barbra. Following their recommendations, I began reading about other professionals who quite unexpectedly began to have afterlife connections with their loved ones. The more I read, the more supported I felt. I soon began to feel I was in good company. They had the courage to talk about their experiences personally and professionally, which not only validated my experiences, but helped me feel I now had a few kindred spirits on my side. For the first time, I breathed a sigh of relief.

Once I embarked fully in the practice, I had no problem connecting to Poppy, at the chosen times. I usually went outside, settling under one of my favorite avocado trees, leaning against its solid trunk. Being in nature connected me to the earth; it helped me feel grounded so I could be fully open to listening and receiving his messages. I could see him instantly in my mind's eye, hear him through my heart center, while, at the same time, writing all we discussed. It always felt genuine. From the moment we connected, I felt surrounded by that same amazing quality of love...which was the ultimate reason for me to trust. Sometimes I asked him for advice, sometimes I asked him about his life. No matter what the subject was, I always felt deeply heard and loved by him...something so very new between us. Feeling his constant love began to heal some of my deeper insecurities about men. I felt more confident to be myself around others; I felt more empowered to offer my opinion in spite of opposition. His insights always gave me a new perspective on matters most distressing to me. His support was never-ending. Every time we talked in this way, my life got better. The many years I had wanted to fix his addiction, along with Mom's depression, vanished. Before, I had always had an intellectual understanding of being codependent in this way. Now, the healing went deeper, like a gale-force wind, sweeping out the hidden remnants of many beliefs that no longer served me. I felt spun around, dropped into new territory, suddenly void of this burden. Whether in family relationships or professional ones, I no longer saw achieving peace as solely my responsibility. The falling away of this burden of misplaced responsibility was freeing.

Even so, doubt could suddenly arrive, switching off my certainty like a light. Fears rushed in, reigning supreme. I worried about what others would think. "What would the neighbors think?" was a constant refrain, which also included my family. I was afraid of being shunned or ridiculed. When this fear arose, I would stop writing. How would I integrate something that was, on one hand, so foreign to me, with something that, on the other hand, was so easy and extraordinary?

One day, as I prepared for my usual morning walk, I heard, once again, that inner voice hounding me with the same old question:

Do Poppy and I REALLY have an authentic and true communication together? This time I was ready to listen, no matter what the answer might be. As I walked down our long driveway, I asked Poppy to give me a sign if what we have was real. Repeating the question to myself several times as I embarked, I eventually let it go, being caught up in the wonders of nature. As I came close to finishing my walk, feeling invigorated by the exercise, I suddenly remembered the question I wanted answered.

I stopped looking all around. I was not sure what I was expecting to see, but I still wanted to be open to any change. On a second check, nothing seemed out of place. Feeling a bit disappointed, I remembered that sometimes it takes time to get a sign. With that insight, I let go of my expectations as I began to walk up the driveway. No sooner had I started walking when, off to the edge of the driveway, something caught my eye. When I looked more closely, I could not believe what I saw. Seemingly out of nowhere, perched between the edge of the driveway, mixed in the leaves from our avocado grove, rested an extraordinary feather, unlike any I had seen before. Feathers abound where I live, frequently coming from hawks, crows, owls, an occasional eagle or even smaller birds. But this one was definitely different. It was a pattern I had not seen before, quite long with striations in shades of brown and taupe. I knew it had not been there before I started my walk; something that large would have immediately caught my eye. Once I picked it up, its energy brought chills all over my body. Having come to believe from my Native American teachers that feathers, especially ones from larger birds, are a message from Spirit, I instantly *knew this was Poppy's sign; it was his answer.* My eyes pooled with tears which then slowly slid down my face. For the longest time, I could not even move. I just stood there, holding this precious feather to my heart. I unconsciously bowed my head, for my heart knew I had just experienced something quite remarkable and really…. miraculous. In a flash, my fears dissolved now that I had received physical confirmation. In that moment, without hesitation, I made the leap from doubt to trust. Spirit had fulfilled its promise, a gift to which I was now ready to fully open.

Looking back, I had dismissed the possibility that we would end up communicating like this, with me here and him in spirit, when it had been hard enough, at times, when he was in physical form. We had had mountains to climb; our love had wounding thorns, mostly from the result of his early traumas and alcoholism. There had been many times either one of us could have permanently closed our hearts to the other. We could have harbored bitter resentment, never daring to address it. But miraculously, each in our own way, and in our own time, despite the past, we somehow chose to keep our hearts open as best we could. I began to see something I had never seen before: this arduous journey had really been leading us to discover the power of soul love. This power led us to accept all of ourselves, for better or for worse. It paved the way to discover love in its purest form. I had held the possibility of resolution between us, not knowing what might occur. If we had not received our beautiful message from Spirit just weeks before his passing, I would not have imagined us having what we now have.

Chapter 14

Unprecedented Healing

My life changed in every conceivable way once I fully accepted Spirit's amazing gift. I felt lighter, less conflicted about everyday concerns. I no longer rushed to judgment about my inadequacies. I became more forgiving of myself. In turn, I became more forgiving of those closest to me. I could trust in a deeper way that all would be OK no matter what my fears might tell me in the short-term because I now felt Poppy's unshakable presence and full acceptance of me. He expanded my vision, offering new perspectives about most things. Despite any lingering reservations I might have about the nature of our new relationship, I felt in awe of being gifted in this way. As the weeks passed, we came together, sometimes with an agenda, sometimes not. It did not matter. Every conversation allowed me to see things from a new, expanded viewpoint. Never a moment went by when I did not feel deeply humbled by the extraordinary gift we had been given.

In one of our first conversations together Poppy surprised me when he said:

"You're an extraordinary being; a creature of light. Don't waste your gifts. Struggle isn't necessary. Struggle is the result of non-alignment between head, heart and your soul's purpose."

From that moment on, the concept of struggle became a major focus of discussion for us; we both had this in common. He had struggled in his life, as had his parents. It had not always been visible, but he showed me what had lain underneath, through an image of how he had swum upstream a great deal of the time, fending off the inner demons that told him he was not good enough or smart enough. Most people who knew him would have never realized how deeply ingrained these beliefs were. They saw only his outer accomplishments. Once I understood his meaning, he would flash a picture in my mind's eye showing me where I struggled. Instantly, I could see the futility of my actions; how unresolved anger or frustration had taken me out of alignment with my purpose. As soon as I understood his point, he would show me a better way to be in harmony with my head and heart, using either a singular image or a series of pictures. Integrating these into my life invariably helped me to better flow with my purpose.

To hear him say that I was *"...an extraordinary being; a creature of light,"* reduced me to tears. Not only was he seeing me in a new way, this way was one I had never seen myself. The years of my life when I longed for him to see all of me vanished; the old injury was healed. Now he saw more of me than I could even imagine. It took my breath away.

My heart knew the truth of his words, but as before, my head was stunned by the language he chose to use, for when he had been my dad, he had never used words like *"creature of light,"* or *"non-alignment between head and heart."* He would not have related to this type of language *at all.* He was far more comfortable speaking of things from a scientific view. His rule was that being taken seriously meant being able to always be rational and objective. Countless times, I had felt shamed by him whenever I spoke of things I "knew" (intuitively), but could not present to him in the manner he required, backed by logical and scientific proof. "Come back to me when you have thought this out more clearly and only when you have proof of what you think is true," he would say in a chastising tone. I had raged inside hearing this because, deep down, I knew I would never be able to meet his standards. Besides, I never wanted to follow the rigors of academic debate (which was what I thought he expected). The way I "knew" things did not require proof in the way he insisted. I had become resigned to the fact he would never know me in the deepest ways...until now.

Knowing this, he admitted, *"I didn't understand alignment as I do now. Emotional pain was crippling. I tried to overcome through my head; my heart was injured. I saw this later. I started to understand more of my soul's purpose just before I died."*

In a flash, I felt the enormity of what he revealed in those brief statements. Things my head never knew yet my heart could definitely confirm. Disowned feelings had interfered with his true alignment. What he said now resonated with how I had experienced him in our very early years; I had never thought of alignment as being the issue.

I usually prepared myself for our connections by being somewhere in nature, for early on he had said, *"Utilize all of nature for balance, peace, and acceptance. You are at home here more than anywhere else."*

I typically had a number of questions for him about work or relationships. Sometimes I asked how to better my work as a psychologist. I also wanted his perspective on how to manage several family matters that were rife with conflict. No matter what I asked, he always focused on the importance of setting my intention first and foremost. He always gave examples I could relate to in order to understand his point.

"A tree with intention grows straight towards the light." he said. *"If you can't see the light, you must have faith; trust from within. Don't let your head be undisciplined by constant thought. Slow and steady. Slow and steady."* His guidance came from his familiarity with my tendency to obsess about work or relationship concerns; I was prone to ruminating for days. This direction was the discipline I needed for my fretting: have faith even though I might not see light. Trust my inner knowing.

The depth and breadth of his expanded vision was uncanny. When he saw how disheartened I had become during his drinking years, he offered this:

"I couldn't nurture all of your energies; I was immersed in my own struggles. I saw only a sliver of you. I understand your anger and frustration with me. I had my own pain. I couldn't be available like now. My work and my healing are to be with you in this way now."

I had never realized that becoming disheartened had had its roots in his emotional absence as I was growing up. For much of my life it was my default position whenever a relationship became conflicted, offering little hope of resolution. Now, his FULL presence allowed me to let out a deep sigh of relief, knowing, for the first time in my life, that he would be an emotional safety net for me.

Poppy's loving presence provided the foundation for my healing. Rarely did he fail to mention how deeply important our conversations were for his healing, as well. In his more expanded form (without ego or personality), I realized he was giving to me in ways he had not been able to when he had been in physical form.

My heart always knew exactly what he was teaching, and it became common to be surrounded in the most amazing quality of love. No matter how slow I might be at implementing what I was learning, Poppy remained patient and accepting. It was an extraordinary way to learn. I had wondered what it would be like to learn at my own speed, surrounded by total love and full acceptance. Most of my early school years had been all about learning at the speed of the teacher, whose eye had been on what was expected at each grade level. I had kept up, but carried anxiety at not being able to learn fast enough. Some of my graduate school instructors had been exceptions, but, in the end, they, too, expected compulsive compliance. I had tried to imagine how it could be to learn in an environment of love, and absence of criticism, or judgment lurking in the shadows at every turn. What would it be like to learn in your own time knowing your timing was perfect in every way? No need for defenses. No need to procrastinate because your effort would not be perfect the first time. Just being held in love, forever. What a model this could be for our world.

For the first few months, Poppy always offered the image of a turquoise stone at the end of our discussions. I knew quite a bit about the deeper meaning of stones. I understood turquoise to have healing properties, providing protection for the body and spirit, frequently enhancing communication between the physical and spiritual worlds. I had placed a turquoise stone by his bedside while he was in hospice care next to a favorite hawk feather. At the time, I had felt the energy of these two things would somehow assist in his journey. Now I wanted to know what the image of this beautiful stone meant to him. Why was he giving it to me at this time? He said:

"Turquoise comes from deep within the earth. It is a rich reminder of all that is from the earth. Indians value this for all things; it is a universal symbol for all that is good."

His answer told me all I needed to know. It was easy for me to see that what we now had was just that—ALL GOOD.

During one of the conversations we had later in the process, I shared my fear of losing my openness to this way of being together. I knew I could sabotage what was so positive instead turning it into a struggle, a pattern I was used to. He smiled saying, *"Honey, be a beginner, new eyes, every day."*

That was the message. So simple, so profound. Again, it was OK to be vulnerable each step of the way; there was not a right or wrong way to do anything…just lead with beginner's eyes. I realized that from his own life of struggle, he was now teaching me how to not struggle. It was beautiful to experience.

When I was faced with dilemmas about work, he reminded me of this:

"Be open to your deeper essence; let it guide you. Anything that doesn't bring out your light is not for you."

I began to understand why I had been troubled at my last place of employment; I saw how my light could not shine. I had felt boxed in, needing to comply with what was asked of me. I had been asked to see more clients, to manage more emergencies, to do more outreach on campus. At first, I had accepted the expectations. But over time, I had become unable to pace myself. I had known I was burning out. I had known I would need to leave at some point. However, I had never considered these work-related frustrations from this particular perspective. I saw how I had wanted to please others, doing what was expected of me. I also saw how I had gotten caught up in the minutiae of office politics, often losing my focus. Before hearing this from Poppy, though, I had never thought to assess whether a situation was supporting *my light*—where I shone, what was highest and best for me. The revelation from that moment is now what I lead with whenever I find myself unhappy in a particular situation or relationship.

Speaking of light, one day I asked for Poppy's perspective about my wonderful godparents. He said, *"Dottie,"* (who was still living at the time) *"is pure light. Your godfather, Wickie, was, too. That's why they were/ are in your life. They had more light than your mother and I. We wanted that for you in case something happened to us. Dottie is now learning about the deepest level of trust within, without all of her loved ones available to her."* (Many loved ones in her family, including her beloved husband, had passed.)

How true it was that Dottie had unconditional love for me, especially toward the end of her 96 years of life. She embodied faith like no one I had ever known. Anyone I loved, she loved. It was that simple. A few years before her death, when she asked me to deliver her eulogy, I was deeply honored. When the time came, I felt her by my side as I shared about her life of love and service that touched us all.

One day I approached Poppy about my difficulty trusting most men. I asked him why he had not been able to be there for me when

I was emotionally vulnerable. He said he had been unsteady and uncomfortable in that emotional space. It had been painful for him to go there with me as well as with himself. Then he added:

"Don't take this as a personal injury; you were an exceptional being. I injured you without realizing it. You have taken this to your depth as you would, being sensitive, loving and open. I always felt your love for me. You saw with innocent eyes in such a trusting way. I see I have contaminated your trust (immediately I saw the color black surround his heart). *I must confess my regrets to you. I needed to address my pain. I didn't. My parents were misguided and hurtful; they themselves had been mistreated."*

Hearing this new perspective made it possible for me to gain a deeper understanding of the past, to heal in a way I NEVER thought possible. Just as I internalized what he said, he provided a shimmering silver cape of protection, saying:

"Wear this, letting it protect you from further hurt and disappointment with others. Hold your own presence with yourself at all times and at any cost. This you must do. My love for you is boundless, ever faithful." He no sooner finished talking when we were surrounded in white, yellow and pink light. It felt AMAZING!

For days after each encounter, I felt the powerful impact of our conversations. Everything he said aided my healing. Each time we spoke I rarely knew on what we would focus or how we would heal. I just let go of any expectations, opening my heart to whatever was best for that moment.

One day, as I prepared to talk to him, I went inward. In my mind's eye I found myself in a forest by a sacred pond, a place we often frequented. As I settled in, Poppy appeared. I told him talking in this way gave me great joy. He agreed. He added we were two souls meant to be together, learning from one another and sharing our love. Once said, he immediately noticed I was feeling out of balance due to other issues I carried at the moment. He quickly offered insight: *"You must incorporate spirituality into your life every day. You are meant to be working at a higher, less dense level. Develop a daily practice of spiritual connection. Read, reflect, meditate, set your intention. Remember, your power comes from within."* I struggled to identify my wants and needs. Even when they were known, I failed to make them a priority at times. I was used to putting others' desires before mine. I experienced this dilemma both at home and at work. I knew I was prone to unrealistic expectations of myself. As a result, I would feel irritable, not realizing I was out of alignment with my body, head and heart. One of his loving comments was:

"You've experienced this way of being in your life purposefully. You were to learn from this: to find yourself, to know the depth of pain, how to transform it, to learn acceptance and compassion for your experiences. Once learned, you could apply it to others. I chose cancer as a way to learn this for myself, to accept, to be present, to learn to be."

I was stunned by this perspective about his cancer, although for the first time, it gave me a greater understanding, perhaps a more spiritual one as well, as to the greater meaning contained within the illness for him. I had an awareness that illness could also be rooted in the emotional/psychological realms; I knew that to be true for myself at various times, but I had never thought of Poppy's cancer being of that nature, until now. The fact he had *chosen* it blew me away. However, this perspective also ushered in a deeper way for me to "see" beyond the beliefs that usually confined me.

In his use of imagery, Poppy always found various places in nature to teach me what I needed to learn. It could be a lesson best learned at the ocean, in a cave, at a waterfall, or even from a fallen tree. It could be lessons learned from animals, such as the deer, that teaches one to live in alignment with their surroundings trusting their innate instincts to guide them, or from all that live in the ocean. No matter what, I felt like each lesson was tailor-made for me.

Poppy also was masterful at using light, color, vibration, water or the earth to help my body and spirit heal. One time when I felt especially contaminated by a relative's ongoing abusive behavior, he guided me to first dig a hole as deep as my feelings were about this behavior. In my mind's eye, I dug until the depth of the hole equaled my anger. Once I completed it, he told me to pull up the toxicity still contained in my body. Without any doubt, I followed this instruction by visualizing myself coughing up a substance that looked like thick black tar. Once it filled the hole, I covered it with dirt. Next, he took me to a nearby stream where I followed his direction to bathe in it until I felt fully cleansed. I had held this anger long enough. To realize how this simple technique allowed me to completely exorcise the anger was beyond anything I could have comprehended in the past. Now, I knew it as a powerful tool that freed me up in ways I never thought possible. Poppy had tailored this visualization specifically for this situation. Over the years I have revisited this way of purging anything toxic with similar results.

When Poppy had been in physical form he would have never shown the slightest bit of interest in any type of healing modality, especially visualization. Again, anyone who knew him would have a difficult time believing how he had changed now that he was in spirit. At times, I was one of them. Yet, the shifts I felt were undeniable. My heart was lighter, my body more relaxed. I met challenges with less angst. My heart knew the power of our conversations spoke the truth in the deepest possible ways.

When I celebrated my upcoming birthday by communicating with Poppy, he told me what a joy it was when I was born. In that moment, there were many colors of light around him as he expressed his love for me as well as his exuberance at my birth. I was so touched I started to cry; it was more than I could take in at first. I took a long moment to breathe deeply. Once my feelings settled, he shared this:

"I felt a heart connection with you from the start like nothing else I had experienced. Life was at its best! I've always loved your openness to what you experience; you're so present with your feelings; you always had a depth to you that was enviable to me."

At that moment, even though I loved what he was saying, I felt unworthy of his description. Old patterns had awakened my default position of self-doubt. He held my face in his hands, saying with love: *"Honey, forgive yourself. It's time to let this belief go."* He further added:

"It's so not about this. Eternal love and connection are forever. Imperfections are always present, especially in human experiences. They are important teachers to have as you are learning. Acceptance is key, not what the imperfection is about. You are as you are. Let this be a day of rebirth for you. . . appreciating yourself, approving of all you are. You are such a blessing to me! Like no other. Easy does it as you continue in your life. Since you have such a capacity for depth, let others help you find your way when needed." He knew how I tried to do most things on my own without asking for help or guidance. I was always frustrated in doing so. I rarely let myself wonder if there were mentors or guides who could assist me along the way.

He took me to the forested area where all of my imaginary animal friends lived, a favorite among the places he provided in our times together. I instinctively knew to bathe in the nearby pool of warm water as the animals surrounded me; they live in harmony with all that is, not knowing any other way. The water was soothing as I let myself be fully nurtured by it. With his eternal heart wide open, Poppy added (referring to this setting and what it meant to me):

"This is the day I want to give you; my gift to you!"

This was the all-time perfect gift…being in the beauty of all that nature always offered. He had got it exquisitely right. As my heart opened to his extraordinary love, especially on this day of my birth, the hurt from past birthdays he had either dismissed or ignored dissolved, never to return. What he had not known in human form, in spirit he now embodied.

By the end of this amazing first year we had covered a full range of topics, beginning with the healing of ourselves, to managing money. Trust was now deeply in place allowed me to finally broach the betrayal I felt about our once-shared investment he had liquidated without my knowledge a few months before his death. "What were you thinking, Poppy? I felt devastated by your actions."

"I only thought of myself," he admitted. *"Not having enough money was one of my worst fears. I was blinded by this. I never thought of this as a betrayal to you. It was a means to an end. I now see how I put our precious relationship in jeopardy. I only have love for you. Thank you for being you, in ALL ways."*

Sometimes we talked weekly, sometimes more. His answers to my many questions were brief, with him showing—more than telling—me where to put my focus. I always had more of a felt-sense of what he meant. Trying to use language as we know it here always fell short of what I experienced. Sometimes, I just could not find the right words to convey his meaning even though I always knew what he meant. As I started to incorporate many of the things he suggested along the way, I found a new sense of balance to my life. There still were moments when I was astounded any of this happened, but they were short-lived. I had not only trusted Spirit's promise, I knew beyond any possible doubt, a loved one's death was not only the final separation, but, if truly desired, healing could resume regardless of whether we resided in the physical world or in the world of spirit. It simply did not matter, for love could transcend the boundaries of any dimension.

The first of many journals I used to transcribe my conversations with Poppy along with the feather he had previously sent to confirm our afterlife connection.

Chapter 15

Writing Our Story

Not long after the first year mark of communicating with Poppy, I consulted once again with Barbra Dillenger. I was excited to share about our year of conversations. I knew Barbra would lend a supportive ear. Once I walked into her office and settled into one of the soft overstuffed chairs, I found my mind racing, wondering where to begin. So much had transpired over the course of the year. I had taken many notes about the conversations Poppy and I had had together. But, once again, before I even had time to organize my thoughts, she turned to me saying quite abruptly:

"You know...your dad says he wants to write a book with you!"

I gasped, unable to catch my breath. Silently, I kept repeating what she said, but I could not fathom it. Did she really just say Poppy wants to write a book with me? This was not even remotely what I thought we would talk about today. Nonetheless, there we were, looking at each other, knowing something big had just happened.

Barbra was only telling me what she had *"heard"* from Poppy; she had no prior knowledge from me that we had been communicating in this manner for the past year. She did not need to. She just knew what she had heard. Apparently, it was time to write a book together. I struggled to find my equilibrium, as my head tried to process this unexpected turn. Several issues came screaming to the forefront: First, I did not see myself as a writer. I had written many academic papers and articles in the past, *but a book?* I did not have the faintest idea where to start even if I wanted to write a book. Next came the question of what we would write about. If we were to write about our conversations from spirit, I was quite protective: they were highly personal and I considered them to be private. Going public with this way of communicating was a giant fear. I would have to "come out" of the spiritual closet, so to speak. The matter of writing a book certainly took me to my edge; the idea of letting others in on this put me into freefall. Talk about fear of the unknown! It enveloped me, momentarily freezing me in my tracks.

For the time being, though, I managed to put aside my shock (and rising fear) to fill Barbra in about the previous year with Poppy by my side. Sharing this returned me to my comfort zone. Barbra listened intently, smiling while appreciating my excitement. She nodded in recognition, knowing how amazing this type of connection is, but once I finished, she was not deterred from pressing her earlier point: a joint book project was around the corner. I was used to knowing how to proceed with most things; however, this idea left me clueless.

On the drive home my fears barged in to scatter my thoughts. I had just gotten comfortable with what had transpired in the past year. Now, something completely unanticipated had dislodged that comfort. I focused on my breathing, letting each inhalation and exhalation settle my reactions. As my emotions quieted, I realized I had several choices: I could say no to this possibility or I could say not now. Or I could just ask Poppy.

Once I returned home, I took myself outside to sit under my favorite avocado tree. I had my journal, the feather Poppy had magically gifted me with and my turquoise stone in my bag. I took a few deeper breaths, quieting my mind. In less time than it took for me to formulate my question, Poppy became present and open about his intentions.

"Writing our story together will teach me to be present, to lead with my heart and always with love—a way to be with myself and with you. I knew some of this before I died—not like now. This is for you—my gift and commitment to forging a new path together—always in love."

Yet being deeply touched by Poppy's reasons to want to write together did not make the fear or intimidation any less daunting. I felt nauseated. As I was reeling from this possibility, I realized these feelings were noticeably absent for Poppy. All he felt was love. How could that be? I was envious because I was not even close to feeling the same. I needed time to let my emotions settle. I stood up and began to pull the many weeds growing in my avocado grove (a never-ending task). This was a sure way to get grounded. The more weeds I pulled, the more I realized if I were going to consider this undertaking—and that was a big IF—it was painfully obvious that I had some work to do, a lot, in fact; my foundation had to be built on total trust of the unknown. . .*trusting that if this were to be the next step for me and Poppy, all would be provided.*

OK, OK, I said to myself, as I thought about the possibility of this new endeavor. I'll move forward, but only at my own pace. Feeling more secure from having set this condition, over the next few months, I timidly stepped on the path, very slowly entering the waters of writing. Keeping my promise to move at my own pace, I started slowly by dipping a toe or two in the shallow end of the imaginary pool. I entered into deeper waters as I was ready. Over the course of a year or so, all the resources I needed seemed to appear: Jan's unwavering support as my therapist, Judith Matson, a colleague of mine whose new writer's group I joined, my dear friend, Kathy Henrich, herself a published author, who volunteered to mentor me in the early stages of my identity as a writer as well as in the early shaping of this story. Poppy, of course, weighed in with unwavering love and support.

All was good. I realized I had drawn upon the same process I had used when I came to accept the gift Spirit first brought me and Poppy. This time it was accepting our call to write our story together. Month after month, I wrote short vignettes about memories in my life with my dad. They were early attempts to find my voice along with learning to capture the deeper meaning of this story. Each member of my writer's group offered helpful suggestions for improvement in spite of me feeling ill-prepared for the task at hand. Even though my writing slowly improved, there were times I felt writing this story was beyond my capability. Over time, I lost confidence. It was one thing to answer the call to write together, but it was another thing to actually know how to write it. Doubts weighed me down. Fear moved in, and I put the book project on hold, being skeptical of its importance. As soon as I did, I let out a sigh of relief, feeling back in my comfort zone. Nevertheless, I would not be there long before I began to receive sharp wake-up calls—usually in the middle of the night—from Spirit, reassuring me I truly was meant to write this story. I was reassured that whatever I needed would be given. Really? I asked out loud one morning. How can I cope, feeling so vulnerable and inadequate? *"Just trust,"* I was told. I let out one of many deep sighs of resignation.

It took over a year before I fully embraced this WAS to be my journey no matter what it took; I finally realized I could either let go or be dragged, as one Zen proverb suggests. I was on a heroic quest, being called to do something beyond my wildest imagination. So, again in small steps, I began to let go of my fear of the unknown as I entered into all the writing process required of me...which was A LOT. Luckily, from the start, I remembered to follow one of Poppy's earlier directives: to deepen my spiritual practice. So, I sat in stillness. I read. I meditated. I deepened my trust. I listened more to my intuition. I slowly let go of any preconceived plan of how this process should go. I gently let myself be imperfect. I remembered to let myself see with new eyes.

As I started to get my emotional footing with this process, my passion for work as a psychologist suddenly began to wane. It came as a complete surprise. By this time, I had worked for fifteen years in private practice, which had been a natural next step of growth from my previous work as a community college counselor and university staff psychologist. I had loved my work. But now, after all the years of feeling so passionate, I felt strangely pulled away from all of it. At first, I did not let this waning interest in work deter me. Strangely, though, I found no matter how much I thought I could focus on both endeavors, I would get a message from Spirit saying, *"Time to move on, dear one; this is not to be."* Being practical by nature, I was not convinced I was ready to let go of what I knew and loved, or if I could let go of my financial base. The more I voiced it to my husband Ken, the more I knew the answer. No matter how out-there or crazy it seemed, my heart clearly knew to follow Spirit's call. I took a very deep breath and trusted.

With Ken's blessing, I took another leap of faith as I lovingly closed my practice, wishing my clients the best. It was the end of a significant chapter in my life that had given much joy. And, as Poppy was fond of saying:

"Appreciate the gifts you've been given for your soul's journey; new ones may appear along the way. Deepen your love for yourself and all else will follow."

I could see I was being given new gifts for this next part of my journey; a greater capacity to listen to and blindly trust my heart was one of them. The more I trusted, the more solid my footing became. Foundational to this approach was my knowing of how Poppy had been right when he suggested deepening my love for myself, first and foremost. When I wondered how to start, the answer arrived instantaneously: *"Keep a gratitude journal."* Every day I noted what I appreciated in myself along with the things for which I was most grateful. Each step I took toward trusting led to greater confidence. Again, the right people showed up as I was ready. One day during a phone consultation with my writing mentor-friend Kathy, she mentioned an online program focused on writing, publishing and marketing your book. She had listened to it the previous year, finding it quite helpful. I took her advice. It was there I was introduced to Christine Kloser, who specialized in mentoring and coaching those who had transformational stories to write. I took a leap of faith (with Mom surprising me by stepping in lending her powerful support for this next step) when I signed on to be part of her author community. I had no rational reason why I signed on (part of me wanted to still believe I could do this all on my own), but I blindly trusted this as my next step, keeping Mom's support close by.

I joined Christine's MasterHeart Program in 2014 by writing and publishing a condensed version of my journey with Poppy in a 2015 anthology entitled, *Pebbles in the Pond, Wave Four.* She valued my story. She encouraged me to step into my light. She nurtured me, as she did many other writers. As a result, I found my deeper story. She was not known as a transformational catalyst for writers by happenstance. She truly knows how to support one's calling. Christine has been by my side ever since, as I participated in some of her key programs. As I look back, I see how she was the perfect person for me to connect with, no matter how irrational it might have seemed in the beginning. I trusted Mom's directive, finally realizing I did not need logic to validate my decision; my heart knew the way through using its own form of logic.

One day as Poppy and I were communicating about how we wanted to shape this story, I found I wanted to know more about the purpose of his alcoholic years since I still saw alcoholism as a complete waste of one's life. He candidly replied:

"Honey, you need to know I chose this path as a way to learn what I needed to learn. I knew my kinship family struggled with alcoholism before I was born; I knew my parents and grandfather chose this path as a way to learn. I knew other family members would be challenged, as well. I wanted to face this challenge. I wanted to overcome it."

Hearing this shocked me! I could not imagine this being remotely the case. Yet the intention behind his words rang true. Everything he had ever said to me had resonated with truth. Early on, Poppy had taught me once anyone transitioned to spirit, truth was the only language spoken. For weeks, my mind cycled through the many crazy, sad and intolerable experiences I had during his years of actively drinking. I always came back to this question: how could anyone choose that? The whole idea was jarring, not a possibility that fit with any of my beliefs. Knowing this, Poppy brought new beliefs from spirit for me to ponder. He showed me how the soul of each person would incorporate lessons and challenges into each lifetime for its own evolution. I felt the expansiveness of his presence no longer living in the confined space of a body. He could be with me in an instant if I requested it. But I was struck by his latest admission.

"OK, Poppy," I said one day in frustration, "I need you to say more about the choice your soul made to experience addiction and recovery."

"*Of course.*"

Instead of telling me, he showed me the many lessons he had come here to learn. It was like watching his life in slow motion, seeing the lesson in every challenge he faced. He showed me how each lesson built on the next. Without one, he could not have the next one. I began to understand.

"Poppy, if you chose addiction as a way to learn certain things, does that mean I (my soul) somehow also chose it as a way to learn?"

He looked at me with incredible love emanating around him, saying nothing. I knew what his silence meant: the answer was yes. I sat in disbelief for days. I tried on the idea. Each time I did, I began to see how it made sense. I saw turning points in my life, as a result of Poppy's alcoholism, that put me on my path as a therapist and a healer. I saw how I was able to impart what I had learned to others new to the experience of living with addiction. In time, I realized that I, too, chose to come from an alcoholic family as a way to learn the many valuable lessons it offered, like assertiveness, self-care, determination, hope, trust, forgiveness, compassion...and the list went on. Once I got past my shock, the symmetry found within the many experiences I had undergone gave me a new perspective altogether. It was quite an awakening!

Being on this spiritual path since the mid-1990s continues to be a constant awakening for me. Being open to Poppy expanded to include other loved ones in spirit once I committed to writing this story. Not long after Mom transitioned, I felt her presence at times, but we did not have an ongoing communication the way I did with Poppy. That changed as soon as I set foot on this path, as she was an ever-present support. Whenever I asked a question involving her, she was instantly present. She shared her experiences of what it was like living with Poppy's addiction when I asked her. I incorporated much of what she said into the story.

My first introduction to Charlie and Alta's voices came as a download of sorrow. This happened while driving home from my monthly writer's group meeting as I was trying to figure out how to incorporate more of my voice into the beginning of the story. How could I do that, not knowing what had transpired between Charlie and Alta? In that instant it came...an immense amount of sorrow flooded my body. I found I could not stop crying. From where was this coming? I no sooner asked the question when I got an answer: the sorrow belonged to my grandparents. Once I got home, I immediately wrote all they shared. First, however, I had to remind them to speak one at a time. They had so much to share they were talking over one another, making it very hard to follow. When they began to take turns communicating, I realized they each held so much sadness. It was heartbreaking. It brought me to my knees hearing about their numerous disappointments and struggles. Their unhealed emotional wounds had remained with them all these years, still unattended. They had been trapped in their human lives and remained trapped now, without any way to make amends to those they had hurt most. They were so appreciative I was open to hearing them, being able to be their voice. Once they finished, I lit a candle as a way to bring them light and love. I said my heart would remain open to anything further they cared to share.

I contacted Uncle Sim and Grandmother Rebecca, asking for their permission to include them in the story. They lovingly offered their insights. Poppy's siblings were enthusiastically on board, as well.

Later, these Culley relatives told me opening my heart offered them the opportunity to speak, accelerating their healing exponentially. That made sense to me. As I mentioned in the introduction to this story some of my past Native American teachings taught me that every time we choose to heal a part of ourselves, we heal our kinship family seven years into the past and seven years into the future. In other words, whatever I heal affects my family as well as my extended family's healing.

Writing this story has brought the opportunity for me to heal in ways I *never* imagined. Maybe that was part of the reason Spirit brought Poppy and I together in this new way...the promise of our soul love? Poppy's intent was clear from the start: to practice being

232

present, lead with his heart, bring love and foster self-acceptance. On the other hand, I was not sure about my own intentions. Later, I realized part of Spirit's promise was to help me step into fully accepting my calling as a translator—a medium—for those who are in spirit; to use my voice as a conduit for those in spirit to share their messages to their loved ones here.

I used to think once someone died, so did any further contact. Now, I clearly know this is not true. Love endures no matter what form we may be in. With a willing heart, healing can always happen.

Poppy lived up to his commitment to be present, leading with his heartfelt love as we wrote this story. It has been an extraordinary gift to feel his ongoing presence in this way. I was even more touched when he asked me to share about his transition to spirit, something I knew he wanted me to write about, but for which we had not as yet set the intention for until now. With my note pad and pen nearby, I lit a candle, settling into a meditative state. I opened my heart to his forthcoming message about his experience before and after death:

"The closer I approached death, the more my mind expanded. I could hear and see things beyond my physical ability. I heard you reading to yourself even though you didn't know I did. My excitement about this made me wake up that evening telling you just that. I wanted you to know I could hear your thoughts in this new way. When we got the message from Spirit informing us of a continuation of our relationship once I left my body, I had already been getting messages from Spirit. I was offered new ways of seeing my life, its purpose and path. It all began to make sense. I knew you knew I was more out of my body than in, towards the end. I could feel your occasional anxiety or sadness, anticipating my departure. I wanted you to see with higher vision. The meditations you read helped you in this way, but I also knew all the emotions you felt were a necessary part of your path. I was in Light a lot. I felt weightless at times. When I would return to my

body I would feel its pain. I learned to see the pain for what it was and surrender to it. You knew Mom was at the foot of my bed at times urging me to leave my body. I knew it too, but I wasn't ready. I was opening to heal in the physical what I hadn't been able to before. I didn't want to leave Corrine this soon; she had been abandoned before. I struggled with this. Light from Spirit showed me how this was part of her path. This allowed me to let go. I crossed over not long after you left that evening. You were right, we had healed all we could. We had clean hands and clear hearts as your Native American teacher, Raven, had taught you. I felt the presence of Jesus show me the way. The moment he touched me, my failures were forgiven. The Light He guided me through was extraordinary, many colors surrounded me, I was weightless. No longer burdened. I was held in this special light for a while to detox from the morphine, as my energy seemed to be everywhere. When you returned that night, the light you felt and saw was my expanded essence lingering in the living room. I was there with you and at the same time, I was elsewhere, too. Any intention I had instantly materialized. I thought of Mom and she was there. I thought of my siblings and they were there, also. My thoughts lingered longer with my parents for we had more healing to do. In the end, I was finally home."

With that said, here are Poppy's parting words…

"Oh, honey, hasn't this been a glorious experience together?! You've done so much to bring this story to light. You've listened. You've been open. You've trusted. You've healed along the way. It's so important for others to know healing is always possible. I say to others: Don't wait another moment to bring light into your life. Life is to be lived in love and joy. Not in fear and sorrow. Fear and sorrow are just some of the temporary teachers our souls bring to us as a way for us to learn a deeper lesson. Find the deeper meaning. Heal. Then surrender to all that is good within and without. Remember, it's ALL good."

Many blessings to you all.

Connecting to
Loved Ones in Spirit

When I share I connect with those in spirit, people oftentimes say they have no experience with this. This may be true. However, I say most people, when given a safe environment to share, realize they have indeed received messages from their loved ones who have crossed over.

I think our loved ones know what is meaningful to us. Poppy knew the importance of feathers in my life; my home has always been filled with them. I believe he "directed" the amazing feather my way the morning I asked him for a sign; he knew it was the perfect messenger for me.

With everyone we love we have a bond; we share similar likes and dislikes; we know which little things are meaningful to them. These things remain true no matter if our loved ones are here physically or in spirit. Once people feel safe to share, I learn amazing things: a book falling off a shelf guiding them to what they needed to know; hummingbirds appearing every time they thought about their deceased daughter or mother; a penny on the sidewalk (once a shared expression of love before death) showing up every time the loved one was remembered.

The moment Ken and I received the news his mother had passed away, a glass shelf in our dining room cabinet suddenly split in half, with a loud crack, making all the glassware it held slide to the end of the shelf. Once inspected, not one item was broken other than the shelf. The glassware had originally belonged to Ken's grandmother. Knowing how much we enjoyed it, his mom passed it on to us over the years. It was definitely her way of making her presence felt at the moment of her passing—and very much in keeping with her strong personality.

My dear mentor-friend, Kathy, upon realizing she had ovarian cancer, told me she would give me a big sign once it was time for her transition. That she did. After arriving home from a holiday trip with my family, I checked emails only to read the one I had hoped I would never get…the news from her husband that Kathy had passed the night before. I went to bed that night feeling deeply sad; I could not bear to think she would no longer be in my life. Furthermore, she would not be here when this book was finished. I lit a candle for her and went to sleep. The next day a neighbor who had been checking our house and property while we were gone called to tell me something strange had happened the day before we returned home. She found a dead hawk laying on top of our pool cover, a very unusual occurrence any time especially in the winter. She had picked it up, putting it out of harm's way. Knowing me as she did, she knew this brought a message of some kind. She did not realize Kathy had passed at the very time she found the hawk. When I shared this story with her husband, he said, "Kathy made a coast to coast fly-by," flying from the east coast where she had lived to the west coast to my home. Once I found the bird, I held its body in my hands noticing there was not a single injury anywhere...nothing! There was not any obvious reason this magnificent creature should be dead. But it was. Continuing to hold the hawk's body close to my heart, I heard Kathy's message:

"I told you I would give you a sign. This is it. I'm free. I'm so very happy. Please take feathers from the wings and the tail. Make an arrangement for you and for our Goddess sisters (which included me and two other women friends); *this will bind us together in spirit."*

As I shared earlier, I never thought I would have an afterlife connection with Poppy, or anyone for that matter. For years, I never thought of myself being sensitive to energies around me, having premonitions, or being psychic despite my ongoing interest in this area. I had been collecting books on these and other metaphysical subjects since the 1980s, now an obvious sign I was being guided all along to pursue this path and accept my calling as a writer and translator for those in spirit.

Many people ask how to be open to connecting with a loved one in spirit. I find it is all about *trust* followed by having an *open heart*. Once these are in place, I do not think there is any one "right way" to approach it. Just the way that feels right to you.

What always feels right for me is to be in nature (depending on the weather); my vibration is higher and lighter when I am among trees. I have a favorite tree I sit under just for this type of communication.

I have a journal dedicated for this purpose that has been sanctified. This sanctifying ritual was taught to me by Barbra. She instructed me to place my dedicated journal on a piece of fabric of my choice, to light two candles that will burn for 12-24 hours beginning at the hour of my birth. (Make sure the candles are of good quality to last the allotted amount of time.) She suggested I tie ribbons which reflect the colors of my vibration or aura (usually blue and purple for me) to the binding of my journal or place them somewhere in the open journal. Next, place the pen I want to use on top of the journal. Last, place a flower across the pages of the open journal. I let the candles burn for the allotted amount of time. Once completed, I place my pen and journal in a special bag which I can carry with me wherever I choose to go. If weather does not permit me to be outside, I have a favorite room in the house that has large windows which provide a lot of natural light.

The suggested layout to sanctify your spiritual journal writings.

I quiet my mind by taking several deep breaths while letting my body relax. Once relaxed, I set my intention: to communicate with Poppy, for example, in the highest and best way. I ask Spirit to protect me, and surround me in Light as we communicate. I always commit to being with him, or others, in this way, using any or all we talk about only for the highest and best good.

I wait in silence, having *no expectations*. I stay open to whatever happens. Often, I receive a picture or an image of what is most important for me to see or hear at the time. With Poppy, I usually "see" him in a place of nature. Sometimes I have questions. Sometimes he wants me to hear something he thinks is important. I am able to write while together without losing focus. Because my vibration is quite different than his at the beginning, I have to wait for his message to make sense to me. In time, our frequencies begin to match, making communication easier.

I know I am in the world of spirit because my energy is lighter. In addition, I am surrounded by an extraordinary presence of love. My heart opens fully without further instruction. It is such an incredible experience. I remember most, if not all, of what transpires. Afterwards, my heart is always full of joy. No matter how I might be surprised by the initial messages, my perspective is always expanded beyond any constraints my ego might have previously put in place. Like most things, it takes practice. There is not any one way to proceed, only the way that is best for you.

Any time I feel a loved one in spirit needs healing, I always light a candle, sending my wishes for healing all that is in their highest and best interest. The healing process starts working instantaneously. In a matter of moments, I usually get a message of deep appreciation.

At first, I did not expect this gesture to have the power it did. Now, I know differently.

Maybe communicating the way I have described is not comfortable for you. Never underestimate the power of simply writing a letter to your loved one, once you've lit a candle, while setting a clear and loving intention. Thoughts are effortlessly transmitted from us to those in spirit, sometimes without us fully realizing it. Write about what upset you the most, then ask your loved one for their insight. You may be quite surprised by what happens next. Maybe you hear a word or phrase, words from a song spring to mind, or you see an image of the person you want to contact. Maybe they point to something for you to see. You may have a very clear feeling about what they are wanting to communicate while not seeing anything else. Just go with your experience, letting it lead you to more.

If your relationship with a loved one was not so loving at times, do not hesitate to seek guidance from a professional. Heal your wounds. Heal your life. As I have learned, every time we heal a part of ourselves, we help heal our loved ones in spirit. Often, loved ones who behaved in unloving ways while in the physical are quite different once in spirit. I have found they can be very willing to make amends if given the opportunity.

I have always surrounded myself with the fragrance of essential oils and the light of a candle, if I am inside. While writing this book I diffused the essential oils of "Valor" or "Peace and Calming" (products from Young Living Oils). If emotion were deeply stirred up, I reached for the essential oil called "Palo Santo."

Reading books written by other psychics and mediums always helped support my process. You may find a favorite one or two from the list I have provided at the end of the book.

No matter what calls you, whether it is similar to my calling, or one completely different, always remember to value your own healing above all else. As Poppy says, *"Your life is meant to be lived in joy and love, not pain and sorrow."* See your challenges as stepping stones to healing that which is meant to be healed. Do not think you can run away from who you are or from how you have been shaped by these challenges. Integrate the past with the present. Use it as your springboard toward living a more joyful life. It is yours for the taking!

Wishing you love and blessings on your healing journey...

Guide For Further Reading

These are books I found helpful along the way...

Alexander, Eben. *Proof of Heaven.* New York: Simon & Schuster, 2012.

Beattie, Melody. *Codependent No More.* New York: Harper & Row, 1987.

Beattie, Melody. *Beyond Codependency.* Hazelden Foundation, 1989.

Beattie, Melody. *The Lessons of Love.* HarperCollins, 1994.

Beattie, Melody. *Stop Being Mean to Yourself.* Hazelden Foundation, 1997.

Beattie, Melody. *Finding Your Way Home.* HarperCollins. 1998.

Black, Claudia. *It Will Never Happen to Me.* New York: Ballantine Books, 1987.

Black, Claudia. *It's Never Too Late to Have a Happy Childhood*. Ballantine Books, 1989.

Black, Claudia. *Changing Course: Healing from Loss, Abandonment and Fear*. Hazelden Publishing, 2002.

Courage to Change, One Day at a Time in Al-Anon II. Virginia Beach, VA: 1992.

Ericsson, Stephanie. *Companion Through the Darkness*. HarperCollins, 1993.

Greer, Jane. *The Afterlife Connection*. New York: St. Martin's Press, 2003.

Holland, John. *Bridging Two Realms*. Carlsbad, CA: Hay House. 2018.

Katye Anna & Allan Sethius. *Soul Love Never Ends*. York, PA: Transformation Books, 2015.

Kennedy, Alexandra. *Losing a Parent*. New York: HarperCollins, 1991.

Kloser, Christine. *A Daily Dose of Love*. York, PA: Transformation Books. 2012.

Levine, Stephen. *Healing into Life and Death*. New York: Doubleday, 1984.

Levine, Stephen. *Who Dies?* New York: Doubleday, 1982, 1989.

Orloff, Judith. *Second Sight*. New York: Warner Books, 1996.

Richardson, Cheryl. *The Unmistakable Touch of Grace*. New York: Simon & Schuster, 2005.

Richardson, Cheryl. *The Art of Extreme Self-Care.* Hay House, 2009.

Santos, Eileen Anumani. *Unmasking Your Soul.* York, PA: Transformation Books, 2016

Van Praagh, James. *Talking to Heaven.* Signet Books, 1977.

About the Author

After retiring from a successful 40-year career as an educator, counselor and psychologist, Pam Culley-McCullough, Ed.D., answered the call from her dad in spirit to write this book, *The Promise of Soul Love, Unexpected Gifts From Here and Beyond.*
She believes every challenge is meant to be a teacher. Once the deeper message is realized, healing relationships with loved ones not only here, but in spirit, can continue.

Pam became a best-selling author when she first wrote about her healing journey as a contributing author in the international best-selling book, *Pebbles in the Pond, Wave Four*
published in 2015. The story entitled, "The Gold in the Darkness," was a condensed version of her journey through her dad's alcoholism and recovery, their healing, and eventual afterlife connection. Navigating this journey brought the deep understanding that each challenge had allowed her to see the "gold" hiding behind the pain.

While writing *The Promise of Soul Love*, she unexpectedly received messages from others in spirit urging her to embrace her next calling... becoming a communicator for those who have completed their transition and long to connect with their loved ones here. She welcomes and honors this new path as a way to help others not only challenge old beliefs they may hold about life and death, but to invite in and foster healing between loved ones here and in spirit.

Pam blogs with her dad, Poppy, and others in spirit, sharing their many valuable insights. You can access her writing at www.conversationswithpoppy.com and are welcome to join her community. Should you wish to begin your healing journey with a loved one in spirit, you can access the meditations provided on her website. If you would like to contact her to facilitate communication between you and a passed loved one, or to schedule a speaking engagement, you may reach her at pam@pamcmc.com.

Pam received her Doctorate from the University of Oregon in Counseling Psychology, her Master's degree in Guidance and Counseling from The College of William and Mary, and her Bachelor's degree in Home Economics Education from Oregon State University.

When Pam isn't writing, consulting or speaking, she can be found scuba diving in tropical waters with her adventurous husband, practicing yoga, walking in her peaceful avocado grove, or singing in her favorite chorale. She greatly enjoys family get-togethers with her two stepsons, their wives and six grandchildren, as well as officiating at weddings for family and friends. She resides in North San Diego County.

Will you post a review on Amazon? If you like what you read in *The Promise of Soul Love,* I'd greatly appreciate it if you'd post a review on Amazon. This will help me reach more people. Thank you! Go here to post your review: thepromiseofsoullove.com

Acknowledgements

The writing of this book required absolute trust and commitment to become what I needed to in order to create the story. And with this tall order, I relied on countless others to support me during the process... many here on the Earth plane while others in Spirit joined in from their dimension, only too happy to assist when needed.

Without my dear Poppy, none of this would have happened. Thank you, Poppy, for always surrounding me in your love, whispering an encouraging word whenever I needed it (which was often!), and being my partner in the creation of our story. I am forever changed as a result. You knew long before I did that I was meant to become a healer for our extended family. Thank you for your steady hand, for insisting I listen to my heart no matter how unnerving it was.

To my incredible Mom who directed me to the right people at the right time. Once I committed to becoming a writer and author,

I wouldn't have found my way without your guidance. You led my team of "ghostwriters," as I affectionately called them, to light my way as I encountered many forks on the road of writing this book. Your support was unwavering and clear, your love endless.

My godparents, Dottie and Wickie, were always my beacon of light leading me to my calling. Thank you for your constant supply of unconditional love while here and in spirit.

To my extended Culley family in spirit... I never thought I would be privileged to know you in the way I now do. Thank you for your confidence in me and your willingness to share your heartfelt stories. I've healed as a result. And I'm humbled to know you have as well.

Healing through my own trauma could never have happened without the expertise, support and compassion from my long-time therapist, Dr. Jan Berlin. His guidance in helping me heal my deepest sorrows enlivened the black and white of my emotional existence to Technicolor.

To my dear friends who mentored me while here and continued to once in spirit, thank you for being part of my "ghostwriting" team. Kathy Heinrich, I miss you more than ever, but our connection remains. You nourished and supported my early years of writing. Without you as my mentor, I wouldn't be where I am now. To Savannah Sincoff, one of the original members of my Writer's Group, thank you for continuing to be your usual wise and spirited self once you passed. Your presence always lifts my spirits.

To Judith Matson, Ph.D., my colleague and friend, thank you for your vision of starting the Writer's Group I've been a part of for the past 12 years. Without that chance meeting at a continuing education workshop, I wouldn't have known of your plans to usher in such a group where I could feel safe to share my early writings. Members of this group have included Judith, Nancy Burnett, June Gottlieb, Randy Hoffman, Ingrid Hoffmeister, Amy Ramaker and Savannah Sincoff.

To my spiritual teacher and mentor, Katye Anna Clark, thank you for sharing your unbridled love and connection to the angelic realm. It introduced me to a new level of support and guidance, one that kept vigil over me every day that I wrote. Thank you for holding the vision my soul had for me that you easily saw five years ago when we met. I deeply value your insight as a seer and teacher of soul.

To my team of holistic physical healers (and you know who you are)... thank you for lending your expertise to amend the mercurial emotional and physical process that writing a memoir invokes. I often needed help to regain my footing and all of you were there to assist.

To my many friends who witnessed the budding of this story from years ago... thank you for staying by my side week-in and week-out as I grew into who I needed to become to write it. Thank you, Sherry Harwell, Mary Jo Barend and Ginger Gibbs for weathering the process with me. A special thank you to my forever-friend, Carolyn Johnson, who heard more than she probably wanted to hear and always offered a solution wrapped in a constant supply of unwavering support. Key parts of the story came together because of you.

To my psychology consulting group, Patricia Heras, Ph.D, Jeff Jones, Ph.D., Jerry Madoff, Ph.D. and John Reis, Ph.D.: our monthly meetings gave me a chance to evolve into my new identity as a writer and communicator for those in spirit. Thank you for offering your support and acceptance to a calling I hadn't expected.

When I selected four friends, all avid readers in their own right, to review my manuscript before entering the publishing phase, these beautiful souls jumped at the chance to offer their insights and suggestions. Thank you, JoAnna DiBernardo, Sharon Hayes, Carolyn Johnson, and Susanne Romo. Every suggestion was priceless and made the story better. All of you gave me the support I needed to forge ahead.

My story would have never found its way to book form without Christine Kloser, a transformational catalyst in the art and science of book writing, and my writing mentor. Thank you, Christine, for believing in this story. You started everything happening on this Earth plane, but I know you were guided by your own amazing team in spirit. Thank you for your intuitive ability to bring out the best in me and this story.

To my MasterHeart family, having an extended support group all started with you as we wrote our stories in the anthology, *Pebbles in the Pond, Wave Four.* What an amazing experience for me!

To my Soul Voyager family created by Christine Kloser, Nancy Baker, Kaylan Daane, Susan Dascenzi, Linda Hyden, Melinda Kapor, Lilia Shoshanna Rae, Linda Roebuck, Susanne Romo, Eileen (Anumani) Santos, Helen Sherry, Julie Stamper, and Kara Stoltenberg, thank you for being my Soul Sisters and holding space for this story to find the light. Poppy made his public debut with you!

Deep-felt gratitude goes to my Capucia Publishing team: Carrie Jareed, who guided me through each step of the publishing process with her special brand of personal and technical support; to my editor, Corinne Dixon, who provided such kind words of support during the lengthy editing phase. You made my story shine. And to Ranilo

Cabo for creating my beautiful cover design. To my photographer, Elsa Rodriquez, for her gift of capturing the best of me. Launching my book into the world would not have happened without the expertise of Viki Winterton and team. Thank you for doing what you do best.

And finally, to Ken, my husband and my life-long love, thank you for being a quiet support from the banks of the river as I navigated the many twists and turns of these uncharted waters. I had a story that insisted on being told no matter how long it might take. Even though it took longer than expected, you stayed steadfast despite the extended timeline. I couldn't have accomplished any of this without your presence, your patience, and your belief in me.

Made in the USA
Middletown, DE
18 October 2020